THE BLACK
DEATH

BUBONIC PLAGUE ATTACKS EUROPE

By Emily Mahoney

Portions of this book originally appeared in *The Black Death* by Don Nardo.

LUCENT
PRESS

Published in 2017 by
Lucent Press, an Imprint of Greenhaven Publishing, LLC
353 3rd Avenue
Suite 255
New York, NY 10010

Designer: Seth Hughes
Editor: Siyavush Saidian

Cataloging-in-Publication Data

Names: Mahoney, Emily.
Title: The Black Death: bubonic plague attacks Europe / Emily Mahoney.
Description: New York : Lucent Press, 2017. | Series: World history | Includes index.
Identifiers: ISBN 9781534560475 (library bound) | ISBN 9781534560482 (ebook)
Subjects: LCSH: Black death–Europe–History–Juvenile literature. | Plague–Europe–History–Juvenile literature. | Epidemics–Juvenile literature.
Classification: LCC RC178.A1 M34 2017 | DDC 614.5'732–dc23

Printed in the United States of America

CPSIA compliance information: Batch #CW17KL: For further information contact Greenhaven Publishing LLC, New York, New York at 1-844-317-7404.

Please visit our website, www.greenhavenpublishing.com. For a free color catalog of all our high-quality books, call toll free 1-844-317-7404 or fax 1-844-317-7405.

contents

Foreword

History books are often filled with names and dates—words and numbers for students to memorize for a test and forget once they move on to another class. However, what history books should be filled with are great stories, because the history of our world is filled with great stories. Love, death, violence, heroism, and betrayal are not just themes found in novels and movie scripts. They are often the driving forces behind major historical events.

When told in a compelling way, fact is often far more interesting—and sometimes far more unbelievable—than fiction. World history is filled with more drama than the best television shows, and all of it really happened. As readers discover the incredible truth behind the triumphs and tragedies that have impacted the world since ancient times, they also come to understand that everything is connected. Historical events do not exist in a vacuum. The stories that shaped world history continue to shape the present and will undoubtedly shape the future.

The titles in this series aim to provide readers with a comprehensive understanding of pivotal events in world history. They are written with a focus on providing readers with multiple perspectives to help them develop an appreciation for the complexity of the study of history. There is no set lens through which history must be viewed, and these titles encourage readers to analyze different viewpoints to understand why a historical figure acted the way they did or why a contemporary scholar wrote what they did about a historical event. In this way, readers are able to sharpen their critical-thinking skills and apply those skills in their history classes. Readers are aided in this pursuit by formally documented quotations and annotated bibliographies, which encourage further research and debate.

Many of these quotations come from carefully selected primary sources, including diaries, public records, and contemporary research and writings. These valuable primary sources help readers hear the voices of those who directly experienced historical events, as well as the voices of biographers and historians who provide a unique perspective on familiar topics. Their voices all help history come alive in a vibrant way.

As students read the titles in this series, they are provided with clear context in the form of maps, timelines, and informative text. These elements give them the basic facts they need to fully appreciate the high drama that is history.

The study of history is difficult at times—not because of all the information that needs to be memorized, but because of the challenging questions it asks us. How could something as horrible as the Holocaust happen? Why would religious leaders use torture during the Inquisition? Why does ISIS have so many followers? The information presented in each title gives readers the tools they need to confront these questions and participate in the debates they inspire.

As we pore over the stories of events and eras that changed the world, we come to understand a simple truth: No one can escape being a part of history. We are not bystanders; we are active participants in the stories that are being created now and will be written about in history books decades and even centuries from now. The titles in this series help readers gain a deeper appreciation for history and a stronger understanding of the connection between the stories of the past and the stories they are part of right now.

SETTING THE SCENE: A TIMELINE

1345-1346 · 1347–1350 · 1361 · · · · · · · ·

A new outbreak of bubonic plague strikes parts of Europe.

The Mongols lay siege to Kaffa, a town on the Crimean peninsula; the attackers catapult plague-infected bodies into the town.

The Black Death arrives in Constantinople, Egypt, Sicily, Italy, the Netherlands, Scotland, Ireland, and Scandinavia.

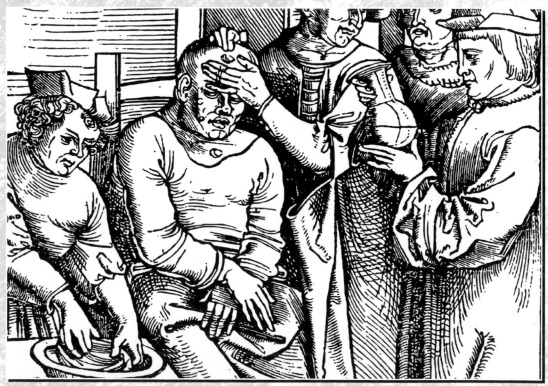

1405–1406	1665–1666	1894	1900–1904

Bubonic plague strikes the U.S. city of San Francisco, where it kills 122 people.

England suffers from its first major outbreak of the plague in the 15th century.

As an outbreak of the plague occurs in China; Swiss scientist Alexandre Yersin identifies the germ that causes the disease.

An unexpected outbreak of the plague kills thousands of London's inhabitants.

A TERRIBLE EVENT IN HISTORY

Italian writer Giovanni Boccaccio is famous for his book, *Decameron*, which was written between 1349 and 1353. "What I have to say is so extraordinary," he wrote, "that if it had not been so often witnessed, and I had not seen it with my own eyes, I could scarcely believe it, let alone write about it."[1] Terrible fear had become so widespread that

> brothers abandoned each other, uncles abandoned their nephews, sisters abandoned their brothers, and wives frequently abandoned their husbands. And there is something else that is almost incredible: fathers and mothers were loath to visit and care for their children, almost as if they did not belong to them.[2]

This frightening recollection is not the product of Boccaccio's imagination.

Rather, his most famous work described one of the worst natural disasters to ever strike humanity. Just two years before he wrote these words, a highly lethal epidemic struck his hometown of Florence, Italy. While Italy tried to handle what has become known as the Black Death, other parts of Europe—Greece, Spain, and other southern European nations—were erupting with the plague themselves. Even people as far away as Palestine, Egypt, and North Africa were showing symptoms of the same disease. In the 14th century alone, the population of Europe was reduced by as much as 60 percent; over 50 million Europeans died in addition to 30 million to 40 million victims in the surrounding areas. Entire villages, towns, and cities were either completely destroyed or significantly depopulated. National economies were left in ruins due to a huge amount of fear and a serious lack of workers. Social, political, and even religious institutions felt the shockwaves produced by the Black Death. Scholars generally agree, historian Robert S. Gottfried wrote,

> that it was not until the mid–sixteenth century that Europe regained its thirteenth-century population levels. And in the late fourteenth and fifteenth centuries, dominated by depopulation and manpower shortages, came changes which profoundly influenced the course of Western history.[3]

At the time, the victims of this biological devastation had no idea what was killing them. Before it was named Black Death, people were calling the disease the Great Pestilence or the Great Mortality. Unfortunately for Europe, the development of germ theory (which is the foundation of modern medicine) was still centuries away. They had no idea that the root of such massive destruction was a tiny microbe (germ) that causes what is now called the bubonic plague. All they really knew was that they were seeing the worst catastrophe in living memory.

SICKNESS IN WRITING

Byzantine historian Procopius described the symptoms of the disease that struck Constantinople (present-day Istanbul, Turkey) in AD 541, which modern science has determined to be the bubonic plague. He wrote,

> With the majority [of victims] it came about that they were seized by the disease without becoming aware of what was coming either through a waking vision or a dream. And they were taken in the following manner. They had a sudden fever … And the body showed no change from its previous colour, nor was it hot as might be expected when attacked by a fever … It was natural, therefore, that not one of those who had contracted the disease expected to die from it. But on the same day in some cases, in others on the following day, and in the rest not many days later, a bubonic swelling developed; and this took place not only in the particular part of the body which is … below the abdomen, but also inside the armpit, and in some cases also beside the ears, and at different points on the thighs.[1]

1. Procopius, *History of the Wars*, trans. H.B. Dewing. Cambridge, MA: Harvard University Press, 1935, pp. 457–458.

Plagues in the Bible

In the centuries leading up to the Black Death, there had been no large-scale outbreaks of serious illness in Europe or the nearby regions. Illness was always a danger in the Middle Ages, but even the worst cases were normally contained quickly. However, the outbreak of the bubonic plague was not the first time that a massive epidemic had affected the fates of entire nations. Indeed, many written accounts of such dire events have survived from past ages.

Some of the oldest of these writings appear in the biblical Old Testament.

Just like 14th-century Europeans, people in ancient times did not know about germs and their role in causing disease. Because sicknesses could kill so many people so quickly, survivors had no way of explaining where they came from. This is partly why the numerous diseases mentioned in the Bible were thought to be punishments from God for things that the people had done wrong. One of the biggest episodes of this type is the large-scale death in the biblical Book of Isaiah. It describes what happened when the Assyrian king Sennacherib laid siege to Jerusalem,

During ancient times, many people believed that widespread disease was God's punishment for their wrongdoings.

capital of the Jewish kingdom of Judah, in 701 BC. According to Isaiah,

Thus says the Lord concerning the king of Assyria:

> *"He shall not come into*
> *this city,*
> *Nor shoot an arrow there,*
> *Nor come before it with shield,*
> *Nor build a siege mound*
> *against it …*
> *For I will defend this city, to*
> *save it …"*

Then the angel of the Lord went out, and killed in the camp of the Assyrians one hundred and eighty-five thousand; and when [the Jews] arose early in the morning, there were the corpses—all dead.[4]

Many historians insist that this story was made up later. It is much more likely that Jerusalem was saved because Sennacherib's soldiers were catching a deadly illness. Canadian American historian William H. McNeill proposed that during the siege, a number of Assyrian troops might have contracted cholera or some other sickness. Eventually, according to this view, their king decided that capturing the city was not worth the effort. In addition, McNeill insisted that the number of deaths seems unrealistic. "The figure of 185,000 disease deaths must be vastly exaggerated," he wrote. "No ancient army came close to such a size, much less one operating in the barren environs of Jerusalem."[5]

Disease Throughout Europe's History

If nothing else, biblical adaptations of disease outbreaks are reminders that such events have often had major historical consequences. According to American military historian Robert Cowley, "Disease has to be counted as one of the wild cards of history, an unforeseen factor that can, in a matter of days or weeks, undo the [most determined plans and efforts] or humble the conquering momentum."[6]

A famous example of disease overwhelming a major military power is the plague that struck the Greek city-state of Athens in 430 BC. At the time, it was one of the two superpowers among the Greek states (each of which viewed itself as a separate nation). The other was Sparta. The Spartans and their allies went to war in 431 BC, and when the Spartans attacked Athenian territory the following year, the Athenians took refuge behind their secure city walls. Then, unexpectedly and with frightening speed, an epidemic struck. The Athenian historian Thucydides, who later wrote a chronicle of the war, described it in these words:

> *People in perfect health suddenly began to have burning feelings in the head. Their eyes became red and inflamed. Inside their mouths there was*

bleeding from the throat and tongue, and the breath became unnatural and unpleasant … Before long, the pain settled on the chest and was accompanied by coughing. Next the stomach was affected, with stomach-aches and with vomiting … The skin was rather reddish and livid, breaking out into small pustules [boils] and ulcers … If people survived this critical period, then the disease descended into the bowels, producing violent … and uncontrollable diarrhea, so that most of them died later as a result of the weakness caused by this. It affected the genitals, fingers, and toes, and many of those who recovered lost the use of these members; some, too, went blind.[7]

The sickness Thucydides described remains unidentified. Whatever it was, it killed at least 25 percent of Athens's residents, including its leading general and politician, Pericles. Many factors contributed to Athens's ultimate defeat in the war, but the loss of the tremendously talented Pericles and so many Athenians to a disease was certainly one of the major causes.

The Greeks were not the only early Europeans who were periodically damaged by epidemics of unknown origins. The Romans had Europe's largest and most powerful empire in ancient times, but they endured three far-reaching and deadly epidemics in the span of fewer than four centuries. The first was probably caused by smallpox or measles. It struck Italy and other parts of the western Roman realm between AD 165 and AD 180. The greatest physician of the age, Galen, estimated that at least a quarter of Italy's population died. The second great disease outbreak—possibly measles or smallpox again—struck between AD 251 and AD 270. At its worst, reports claim that the disease killed up to 5,000 people a day in the city of Rome.

The third and most destructive of the Roman epidemics appeared in AD 541 throughout the eastern Roman sphere (later called the Byzantine Empire). Named after the Byzantine emperor at the time, Justinian, it became known as Justinian's Plague. According to the Byzantine historian Procopius,

During these times there was a [terrible sickness], by which the whole human race came near to being annihilated. Now in the case of all other [plagues] sent from Heaven some explanation of a cause might be given by daring men, such as the many theories [proposed] by those who are clever in these matters … But for this calamity it is quite impossible either to express in words or to conceive in thought any explanation, except indeed to [say the cause is] God.[8]

Justinian's Deadly Plague

Justinian's Plague was particularly notable for three reasons. First, it was extremely widespread. As far west as Ireland and as far east as southern Asia felt its effects. Second, it was horribly lethal. Throughout all of southern Europe, an estimated one-fourth of the total population was killed by the same disease. The third reason the epidemic was significant is that it is the earliest recorded instance of the bubonic plague.

The outbreak of this lethal plague during the 500s gave Europe its first nasty taste of the microbial murderer

Justinian was emperor of Rome when a deadly plague struck.

The bubonic plague killed millions of people throughout Europe and Asia.

that would kill even more Europeans during the great outbreak of the 1300s. However, because 800 years separated the events, those who suffered in the later outbreak had no memory of the earlier one. For that reason, the second epidemic of the Black Death to hit Europe seemed to come with no warning. Most people viewed it as so huge and unique that only God could be responsible for it. That explanation became a major theme of the age. To try to stop the disease, people tried anything to make God happy. The fear of upsetting God would come to define global society for centuries, even when the rise of scientific medicine offered an alternative explanation.

CHAPTER ONE

BLACK DEATH BEGINNINGS

Few events in history have been as devastating as the Black Death in Europe during the 14th century. Looking back, it is easy to see why it had such an impact. There are three main reasons: First, the cause of the Black Death was unknown; second, there was no known cure; third, the European people were simply not prepared to have such a deadly disease sweep through their countries, villages, and homes.

Europe had been lucky in the sense that it had been free of widespread disease for several centuries before the plague spread throughout the continent. Most of the diseases during the time only affected small groups of people. They also tended to be associated with malnutrition, especially during the early medieval era. Malnutrition is when the body is not able to get the right kind of nutrition, and it can cause

many different problems. Sometimes, there were also outbreaks of a disease that was called Saint Anthony's fire, a type of poisoning that is caused by a fungus from rye and other grains (today, it is called ergotism).

Another medieval health concern was leprosy, an infection that can badly damage the appearance of someone's face and limbs. Although leprosy was a frequent concern, it is not very contagious and rarely fatal. Of course these diseases were frightening for the Europeans, but none were nearly as contagious or widespread as the Black Death. This contributed to the mass panic and hysteria caused by the plague when it began to spread and kill quickly.

Another important factor to consider when discussing the huge number of people who were killed by the Black Death is that Europe had many potential victims for the plague to claim.

From the 600s to the early 1300s, when Europe was relatively disease-free, the continent's population increased significantly. It tripled in size during this period, and as a result, Europe had roughly 70 million people by the mid-1300s.

The people were unprepared for the onset of sickness and death on a massive scale and had no idea how horrible disease and its effects could be. When the epidemic began to spread, this ignorance turned into fear. Both death and the unknown were so feared that the structure of civilized life and society broke down. Incidents such as those observed by Boccaccio, of parents abandoning their children and brothers deserting brothers, were repeated countless times across the continent. It is no wonder that even those who lived through the tragedy thought their entire world was coming to an end.

Spreading from Central Asia

Although 14th-century Europeans did not know what caused the Black Death, they did have a good idea of where it came from. Several contemporary writers, including the Italian Gabriel de Mussis, claimed that it entered Europe from "the East." To Europeans, the East was a general term for Asia, including the region now called the Middle East.

Modern experts confirm this assumption. Evidence has been found that suggests bubonic plague bacteria originated far to the east of Europe.

One of the key clues was the 1885 discovery of an old graveyard near the ruins of a medieval Christian community by a large lake in south-central Asia named Issyk Kul. To Europeans, this location would certainly be "the East." In the cemetery, a Russian archaeologist found an abnormally large number of graves that were dug in 1338 and 1339. Additionally, some of the grave markers said that the cause of death was some kind of disease.

Scientists believe that the disease reached the Issyk Kul area from somewhere in central Asia, probably first spreading from animals to humans in that region. According to distinguished medical researcher Alfred J. Bollet,

In this area of Central Asia, marmots [large squirrels] were trapped for their fur, which was then sold to various traders who [shipped] them along [local] caravan routes. Hunters and trappers always were happy to find sick or dying animals that they could catch easily, and around this time many untrapped marmots were found dead; trappers skinned these animals and sent the furs to be shipped to buyers in the West. Bales of marmot fur probably contained living fleas [infected with plague] that became very hungry without a live animal on which to feed ... The furs reached [towns along the trade routes] and, when the bales were opened, the hungry fleas jumped out [and onto humans].[9]

The city of Kaffa, shown in this engraving, is where most modern experts believe the Black Death entered Europe.

From central Asia, modern experts estimate that the disease moved westward along the major trade routes leading to the area near the Black Sea. At the time, much of this western Asian region was ruled by the Mongols (called Tartars by medieval Europeans). By the mid-1340s, many Mongols and others in the area had died of the plague. The next area to be infected was Crimea, a highly populated peninsula to the north of the Black Sea.

There, in the winter of 1345 to 1346, a Mongol leader was attempting to capture the town of Kaffa. Located between the borders of Asia and Europe, Kaffa was a colony of Italian city-state Genoa and one of Europe's great trading centers. The Mongols, however, soon had more to deal with than capturing the town. According to de Mussis, "The whole army was affected by a disease which overran the Tartars and killed thousands upon thousands every day." He added that "All medical advice and attention was useless; the Tartars died as soon as the signs of disease appeared on their bodies."[10] The Mongol leader saw what the unknown ailment was doing to his own soldiers and came up with a plan. Today, what he did is referred to as biological warfare. As noted British scholar Philip Ziegler wrote,

They used their giant catapults to lob over the walls [of Kaffa] the corpses of the [Mongol] victims in the hope that this would spread the disease within the city. As fast as the rotting bodies arrived in their midst the Genoese carried them through the town and dropped them into the sea. But few places are so vulnerable to disease as a besieged city and it was not long before the plague was as active within the city as without.[11]

The European Invasion

Between the Mongolian siege and the increasing sickness, many people were dying inside the town of Kaffa. Those who were still living were desperate to escape. Some people did manage to board ships and sail southward into the Black Sea, but they did not realize that they were carrying this deadly disease with them. They brought the plague first to Constantinople, the mighty Byzantine metropolis on the sea's southern shore. From the dock areas, the disease quickly spread into the city's streets. No neighborhood or building—small or large, rich or poor—was immune. By mid-1347, the plague in Constantinople was an epidemic.

However, much worse was to come. Constantinople was a busy hub for traders from across the Mediterranean-European sphere. Traders and merchants came from all over Europe and Asia to sell their goods in the Byzantine city. When they left, their ships were carrying the disease. This caused the Black Death to move southward into the Mediterranean, bound for ports in Palestine, Egypt, North Africa, Greece, Italy, and beyond. Not long afterward, a Byzantine observer wrote, "A plague attacked almost all the sea coasts of the world and killed most of the people."[12]

Italy was one of first regions to feel the deadly impact. In 1347, 12 vessels carried the plague to the city of Messina in Sicily. Italian writer Michael of Piazza described the initial and crucial outbreak in Messina:

At the beginning of October ... twelve Genoese galleys ... entered the harbour of Messina. In their bones they bore so virulent [potent] a disease that anyone who only spoke to them was seized by a [lethal] illness and in no manner could evade death. The infection spread to everyone who had any contact with the diseased [people] ... Not only all those who had speech with them died, but also those who had touched or used any of their things. When the inhabitants of Messina discovered that this sudden death [came] from the Genoese ships they hurriedly ordered them out of the harbor and town. But the evil remained and caused a fearful outbreak of death.[13]

From Europe's trading ports, the Black Death moved northward and eastward. In Italy, it struck all the urban areas, including Padua, Pisa, Rome, and Florence, with a fury. Michael of Piazza described some of the frightening symptoms:

Those infected felt themselves penetrated by a pain throughout their whole bodies and, so to say, *undermined. Then there developed on the thighs or upper arms a boil about the size of a lentil which the people called "burn boil." This infected the whole body, and penetrated it so that the patient violently vomited blood. This vomiting of blood continued without [stopping] for three days, there being no means of healing it, and then the patient [died].*[14]

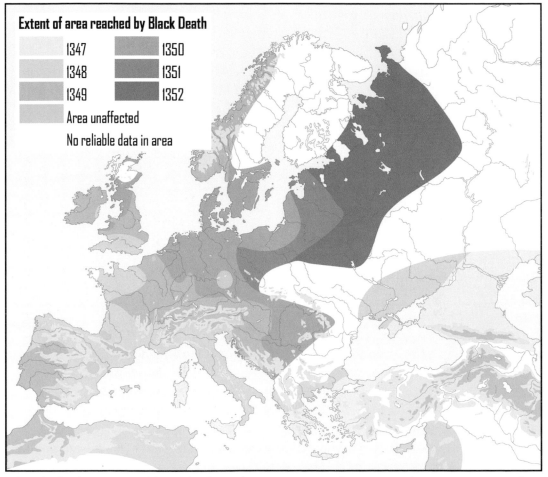

Extent of area reached by Black Death

1347	1350
1348	1351
1349	1352

Area unaffected

No reliable data in area

The Black Plague spread quickly throughout Europe, and many people were unprepared for its far-reaching effects.

MESSINA'S BLACK NIGHTMARE

Italian writer Michael of Piazza described the terrifying spread of the plague through the Italian city of Messina in 1348:

> Soon men hated each other so much that if a son was attacked by the disease his father would not tend him. If, in spite of all, he dared to approach him, he was immediately infected and was bound to die within three days. Nor was this all; all those dwelling in the same house with him, even the cats and other domestic animals, followed him in death. As the number of deaths increased in Messina many desired to confess their sins to the priests and to draw up their last will and testament. But ecclesiastics [clergy], lawyers, and notaries refused to enter the houses of the diseased.
>
> Soon the corpses were lying forsaken in the houses. No ecclesiastic, no son, no father, and no relation dared to enter, but they hired servants with high wages to bury the dead.[1]

1. Quoted in Johannes Nohl, *The Black Death: A Chronicle of the Plague*, trans. C.H. Clarke. London, UK: Allen and Unwin, 1926, p. 19.

The Effects of Death

There were so many victims of the Black Death in each town that the streets were soon full of corpses. Boccaccio's *Decameron* again offers a look into the horror of the Black Plague in Florence, Italy. Many people "finished up [their lives] on the streets," he wrote, "and those who did die in their homes only made their neighbours aware of their death by the stench from their corrupted [decomposing] bodies." He continued,

> The city was full of corpses. Most of them were dealt with in the same way by their neighbours, influenced as much by fear of being infected by the rotting bodies as by charity towards the dead. By themselves, or with the aid of bearers … they dragged the newly dead out of their homes and placed them upon their doorsteps, where anyone who passed by, particularly in the morning, could see countless numbers of them.[15]

Having dead bodies piled up throughout a city was obviously a problem, and Florence was not unique in this regard. Many other European cities began to see their dead pile up.

As the Black Death spread, the bodies of its victims piled up on the streets of almost every European city.

What made this worse was another dilemma—the corpses needed to be removed, but no one wanted to touch them. People feared they might catch the plague through bodily contact or even through being near the corpses at all. As a result, very few were willing to take on the awful task of burying the dead. In most cases, people ended up paying low-class thugs and criminals to do it. According to Boccaccio,

> [F]ew bodies were accompanied to church by more than ten or a dozen of their neighbours, and even these were not respected citizens. Instead, a band of scavengers, drawn from the dregs of society ... bore the bier [coffin]. And they bore it in a hurry, usually not to the church which had been chosen but simply to the nearest [church] ... [and] put the body as quickly as they could into any unoccupied grave.[16]

Still another problem with the masses of infected dead bodies was where to bury them. Most Europeans were Christians and expected to be buried in sacred ground, generally preferring cemeteries next to churches. As Boccaccio wrote,

> There was not enough consecrated [sacred] ground to bury the great multitude [numbers] of corpses arriving at every church every day and almost every hour ... So, when all the graves were occupied, very deep pits were dug in the churchyards, into which the new arrivals were put in [the] hundreds. As they were stowed there, one on top of another, like merchandise in the hold of a ship, each layer was covered with a little earth, until the pit was full.[17]

Mass graves such as this were often called plague pits. However, in some European cities, these pits were not enough. Sometimes the deceased were burned. This was done for two main reasons: There was not enough space, and fire was thought to cleanse infection. Land across Europe, especially land for cemeteries, was difficult to find. Although cremation was a rare choice in medieval times, it was quickly adopted and used throughout Europe for thousands of corpses. In this way, not only were the streets cleared of bodies, but people thought they were reducing their chances of being infected.

An intense fear of death overcame the population, Boccaccio observed. Because people believed they would probably die soon, they started

Bodies were often burned because there was nowhere else to put them or bury them.

behaving with no regard for the rules of society. Maintaining law and order in a diseased land was almost impossible, as governments were more concerned with surviving the plague than the general welfare of their citizens. Feeling compelled to comment on the breakdown of morals and civil behavior he saw occurring around him, Boccaccio wrote,

I have frequently heard of people, and seen them, who make no distinction between right and wrong, but only consider their appetites, and simply do ... whatever gives them most pleasure. I am speaking not only of [average] people, but of monks in their monasteries who, having ... broken their rule of obedience, [have] given themselves over to [corruption], hoping by this means to avoid the plague. If this is true, and it obviously is, what are we doing here, what are we waiting for, what are we thinking of? ... [How] foolish we are, to think like this![18]

Selfishness Spreads

Boccaccio was not the only person who was shocked and disgusted by the growing anarchy across Europe. Other distressed observers witnessed similar instances of selfishness as the epidemic spread northward into the heart of Europe. One was French chronicler Jean de Venette. Describing the

AN UGLY DISEASE

In the year after the Black Death struck the British Isles, a Welsh poet named Jeuan Gethin wrote this lament, which described the unsightly, painful lumps the disease caused on people's bodies:

We see death coming into our midst like black smoke, a plague which cuts off the young, a rootless phantom which has no mercy or fair countenance [good looks]. Woe is me of the shilling [lump] in the arm-pit; it is seething, terrible, wherever it may come, a head that gives pain and causes a loud cry, a burden carried under the arms, a painful angry knob, a white lump. It is of the form of an apple, like the head of an onion, a small boil that spares no-one. Great is its seething, like a burning cinder, a grievous thing of an ashy colour. It is an ugly eruption that comes with unseemly haste. It is a grievous ornament that breaks out in a rash. The early ornaments of black death.[1]

1. Quoted in Mike Ibeji, "Black Death," BBC, March 10, 2011. www.bbc.co.uk/history/british/middle_ages/black_01.shtml.

plague's swift and deadly passage through his native land, he wrote,

Nothing like the great numbers who died in the years 1348 and 1349 has been heard of or seen in times past … If a well man visited the sick he only rarely evaded the risk of death. [As a result] in many towns timid priests withdrew, leaving the exercise of their ministry to such of the religious as were more daring. In many places not two out of twenty remained alive. So high was the [death toll] at the Hôtel-Dieu [hospital] in Paris that for a long time, more than five hundred

dead were carried daily with great devotion in carts to the cemetery of the Holy Innocents in Paris for burial.[19]

The epidemic also struck the French city of Avignon, which was currently the headquarters of the Catholic Church and Pope Clement VI. A leading member of the Church reported, to his horror, that half of Avignon's residents died in the outbreak's first two weeks alone. He further observed,

Within the walls of the city, there are now more than 7,000 houses shut up; in those no one is living, and all who

This depiction of the plague shows what many people feared: They would not make it out of this epidemic alive.

have inhabited them are departed; the suburbs hardly contain any people at all. A field near [the church] "Our Lady of Miracles" has been bought by the Pope and consecrated as a cemetery. In this, from the 13th of March [1348], 11,000 corpses have been buried. This does not include those interred [buried] in the cemetery of the hospital of St. Anthony, in cemeteries belonging to the religious bodies, and in many others which exist in Avignon.[20]

After nearly all of France had been destroyed by the wave of infection,

the disease reached the banks of the English Channel. The English hoped that the wide waterway would protect them from the oncoming natural disaster. This, unfortunately, was not the case. Carried by rats that stowed away on boats, the Black Death leapt across the channel late in 1348. It spread from southern England northward, and less than a year later, after it arrived on England's shores, it reached the Scottish highlands and eastern Ireland.

Rats also stowed away on trading vessels headed to the lands today known as Germany, Poland, and Russia. The Russian city of Moscow

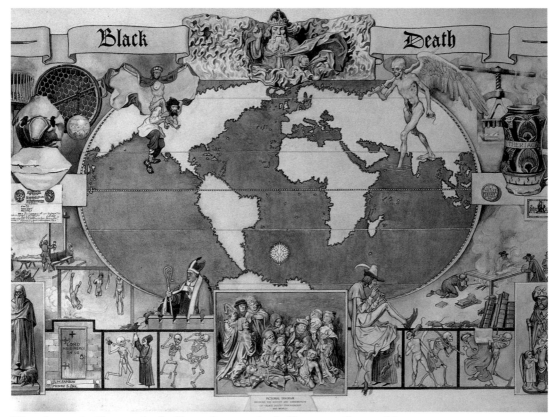

The plague in Europe had effects that reached all across the world.

was devastated between 1352 and 1353. The Russians recorded the same symptoms and high numbers of death of the western European plague. The leader of eastern Russia, Grand Prince Ivanovich, died of the plague and so did many members of his royal family. The Russian regions of "Pskov and Novgorod were repeatedly stricken beginning in 1360 ... [and shut] their gates"[21] in an attempt to stop the continued outbreaks of the Black Death.

Creature Casualties

The Black Death also directly and indirectly affected animals around Europe. With few or no humans left to take care of them in many areas, domestic livestock—including sheep, pigs, goats, chickens, and even oxen—ran wild. Whether roaming free or still under control, many of these beasts died from the plague in the same manner that people did. English chronicler and eyewitness Henry Knighton wrote,

> There was a great murrain [mass death] of sheep everywhere in the kingdom, so that in one place in a single pasture more than 5,000 sheep died; and they putrefied [rotted] so that neither bird nor beast would touch them ... Sheep and cattle ran at large through the fields and among the crops, and there was none to drive them off or herd them; for lack of care they perished in ditches and hedges in incalculable numbers throughout all districts, and none knew what to do.[22]

Large numbers of wild animals also died from the disease. Some that survived could sense that human control was weakening. The most aggressive animals moved into human areas. One troubled observer described the threatening behavior of wolves and other creatures that normally lived in the German woodlands:

> Savage wolves roamed about in packs at night and howled round the walls of the towns. In the villages they did not slake [satisfy] their thirst for human blood by lurking in secret places ... but boldly entered open houses and tore children from their mothers' sides. Indeed, they not only attacked children, but armed men, and overcame them ... They seemed no longer wild animals, but demons. Other creatures forsook [left behind] their woods. [For example] ravens in innumerable flocks flew over the towns with loud croaking. The kite [a bird of prey] and the vulture were heard in the air, [and] on houses the cuckoos and owls alighted [sat down] and filled the night with their mournful lament.[23]

All of these strange and frightening events made people think that something unnatural and horrible was happening. It seemed to be taking place everywhere and affecting all aspects of nature and human society. A native of Siena, Italy, who lost all five of his children to the Black Death, summed up what so many other Europeans thought about the extraordinarily horrific disaster. "No bells tolled [for the dead]," he wrote. "And nobody wept no matter what his loss because almost everyone expected death." He added, "People said and believed, 'This is the end of the world.'"[24]

Life was turned upside down by the plague. Many believed that life would never return to normal because of the mass destruction and devastation.

CHAPTER TWO

A PLAGUE OF
TERROR AND PANIC

People living in Europe had many different reactions to the deadly onset of the great plague in the mid-1300s. Some people became irrational and even violent. Other people searched for omens to see if they had been warned of the terrible disaster ahead of time. An omen is a supernatural sign of major events to come, and many people believed that omens could warn of terrible events coming their way. Others tried to explain what was causing the devastating epidemic, but because science and medicine were not yet advanced enough to explain it, they failed. Some people even reacted by harming themselves or persecuting innocent people because their fear and hysteria were so great.

Strange Theories About the Plague

In ancient and medieval times, it was very common to look for omens before natural disasters, the birth of nobility, or other major events. As a terrible natural disaster, the spread of the Black Death motivated people to look for any signs that had come before the epidemic. Some recalled that strangely heavy mists had blanketed several European regions in 1347. Others remembered seeing falling stars (which are nothing more than tiny meteors burning up in the atmosphere). One sign that many people called attention to was described by Jean de Venette:

In the month of August, 1348, after Vespers [evening worship] when the sun was beginning to set, a big and very bright star appeared above Paris, toward the west. It did not seem, as stars usually do, to be very high above our hemisphere but rather very near. As the sun set and night came on, this star did not seem to me or to many other friars who were watching it to move from one place. At length, when night had come, this big star, to the amazement of all of us who were watching, broke into many different rays and, as it shed these rays over Paris toward the east, totally disappeared and was completely annihilated. Whether it was a comet or not, whether it was composed of airy exhalations and was finally resolved into vapor, I leave to the decision of astronomers. It is, however, possible that it was a presage [omen] of the amazing pestilence to come, which, in fact, followed very shortly in Paris and throughout France and elsewhere.[25]

This drawing shows what a typical plague doctor dressed like as he tried to treat his patients.

Modern scholars think that de Venette and the others witnessed a large meteor that broke into pieces as it raced through the atmosphere. However, comets were not the only strange theory of the plague. For instance, some people suggested that earthquakes had supposedly unleashed foul vapors from deep within the earth, which made humans sick when they inhaled them.

A number of people also blamed the unnatural movements of the planets. They argued that this strange motion had caused the air on Earth to become corrupt and thereby infect humans with terrible sickness. This impure air hypothesis was supported by many intelligent scholars of the day, including noted physicians. In October 1348 a group of French doctors wrote,

[I]llnesses can be caused by the corruption of water or food ... yet we still regard illnesses proceeding from the corruption of the air as much more dangerous. This is because bad air is more noxious [poisonous] than food or drink in that it can penetrate quickly to the heart and lungs to do its damage. We believe that the present epidemic or plague has arisen from air corrupt in its substance, and not changed in its attributes. By which we wish it [to] be understood that air, being pure and clear by nature, can only become putrid or corrupt by being mixed with something else, that is to say, with evil vapours.[26]

Many specialized doctors during this time truly believed that "evil vapours" were the cause of the Black Death. Today, the uniforms these doctors wore are recognizable symbols of the bubonic plague. They wore large hats, stiff cloaks, and bird-like masks. They filled these masks with herbs and flowers that were believed to purify the infected air.

A Furious God

Many reasons were given for the spread of the plague, but none was more widespread than the idea that it was a punishment sent by God. In September 1348 an English priest stated,

Terrible is God toward the sons of men, and by his command all things are subdued to the rule of his will. Those whom he loves he censures [condemns] and chastises [punishes]; that is, he punishes their shameful deeds in various ways during this mortal life so that they might not be condemned eternally. He often allows plagues, miserable famines, conflicts, wars and other forms of suffering to arise, and uses them to terrify and torment men and so drive out their sins. And thus, indeed, the realm of England, because of the growing pride and corruption of its subjects, and their numberless sins ... is to be oppressed by the pestilence.[27]

God was not the only supernatural being blamed for bringing on the plague. Respected scholar of medieval times Barbara W. Tuchman wrote,

Scandinavians believed that a Pest Maiden emerged from the mouth of the dead in the form of a blue flame and flew through the air to infect the next house. In Lithuania the Maiden was said to wave a red scarf through the door or window to let in the pest. One brave man, according to legend, deliberately waited at his open window with drawn sword and, at the fluttering of the scarf, chopped off the hand. He died of his deed, but his village was spared and the scarf [was] long preserved as a relic in the local church.[28]

Restrictions and Laws

These explanations, which seem so strange today, demonstrate the fact that medieval doctors had no clue as to what caused the epidemic. They also did not know how to give any sort of treatment to people who had the disease. On the other hand, it did seem apparent to doctors, as well as many ordinary people, that the plague was somehow contagious. For this reason, a number of towns restricted travel and created rules for public hygiene and quarantines (the separation of plague victims from healthy people). While these new policies were not enough to stop the spread of the Black Death, they undoubtedly helped save some lives.

One well-documented example of anti-plague laws was a decree issued in May 1348 in the Italian town of Pistoia. "No citizen of Pistoia," it said, "shall in any way dare or presume to go to Pisa or Lucca or to the county or district of either."[29] Similarly, no one was allowed to travel from those cities to Pistoia; if they did, they had to pay a hefty fine. Pistoia's rulers also passed laws that regulated the sale of meats and clothing.

Authorities in Venice issued similar rules in 1348. Officials were selected to help maintain public health and hygiene efforts. Additionally, any foreign vessels were required to wait for

Many doctors left during the plague, causing others to view them in an unfavorable light. This drawing depicts a plague doctor as half-chicken.

40 days before they could enter the Venetian harbor. (City officials could not predict how long the epidemic would last. This specific time period was chosen because it is the amount of time the Bible says that Jesus suffered in the wilderness.) Anyone who was sick or was showing symptoms inside the city was taken out to one of Venice's uninhabited islands to be quarantined.

Despite these earnest efforts, the plague killed 100,000 people in Venice, which was roughly 60 percent of its residents. Among the dead were many doctors. Of those physicians who lived, most fled the city and left their patients to suffer in agony. One exception was a doctor named Francesco, who remained at his post throughout the crisis. When asked why he did not run away like his fellow physicians had, he replied, "I would rather die here than live elsewhere."[30]

All across Europe, similar attempts to stop the spread of the plague emerged. These were all largely useless because there was no known cure, and no one realized that the disease was transmitted by fleas and rats. As a result, these disease carriers still came into contact with people and spread the plague.

Who Is to Blame?

Because nothing substantial was known about the causes of the Black Death, many frightened and desperate people searched for someone to take the blame. These scapegoats were almost always viewed as abnormal and lived outside of mainstream society. A surgeon in the French city of Avignon described some of the more common scapegoats whom he witnessed being persecuted:

In some places ... they drove out paupers [poor people] who were deformed, in others they drove out nobles. Things finally [got so bad] that guards were posted to see that no one who was not well known would enter a city or village. And if they found anyone carrying medicinal powders or ointments they would force him to swallow them, to prove that they were not poisonous potions.[31]

Poor people and outsiders were not the only people targeted. Mentally ill and physically impaired people were also frequently suspected. According to scholar James C. Giblin,

On the edges of many villages, in poor huts made of sticks and straw, lived outcasts of various kinds. Some were deformed from birth, others were simple-minded, still others were insane. The villagers gave them names like Poor Tom and Mad Mag. The majority were harmless, although children sometimes taunted them and called the old women witches. Most adults simply left them alone.

That changed when the Black Death came. As more people sickened and

died, the survivors became increasingly frustrated. Neither the village priest nor the barber-surgeon had a solution for the plague ... Maybe the children were right, [many villagers] thought. Maybe Mad Mag really was a witch. If they got rid of her, maybe the pestilence would finally go away.[32]

The biggest group that medieval Europeans blamed for the Black Death was the Jews. They were accused of many things during this time period, including poisoning wells and other supplies of drinking water in order to exterminate Christians. In 1348, an Italian commentator reported that

[s]ome [Jewish] men were found in possession of certain powders and (whether justly or unjustly, God knows) were accused of poisoning the wells—with the result that anxious men now refuse to drink water from wells. Many were burnt for this and are being burnt daily, for it was ordered that they should be punished thus.[33]

Hatred and Distrust

It is only natural to wonder why so many people believed Jews had caused the terrible epidemic. Part of the reason is that Jews had a negative image because of the Bible. Based on traditional Christian teachings, Jews were responsible for the death of Jesus. As a result, most Europeans,

STRANGE COMMANDS

On the long list of plague laws decreed in Pistoia, Italy, were the following:

IX. Item. They [the rulers of Pistoia] have provided and ordered that no paid mourner ... shall dare ... to mourn publicly or privately or to invite other citizens of Pistoia to go to the funeral or to the dead person ...

X. Item. So that the sounds of bells might not depress the infirm nor fear arise in them [the rulers] have provided and ordered that the bellringers or custodians in charge of the belltower of the cathedral of Pistoia shall not permit any bell ... to be rung for the funeral of the dead nor shall any person dare or presume to ring any of these bells on the said occasion ...

XII. Item. They have provided and ordered that no person should dare ... to raise or cause to be raised any wailing or clamor [loud crying] over any person or because of any person who has died outside the city, district or county of Pistoia; nor on the said occasion should any persons be brought together in any place except blood relatives and associates of such a dead person.[1]

1. "Ordinances for Sanitation in a Time of Mortality," Institute for Advanced Technology in the Humanities. www2.iath.virginia.edu/osheim/pistoia.html.

In medieval times, professional mourners were often hired to cry at funerals to set the somber mood.

This drawing from the 14th century shows Jews throwing a baby off a tower to fend off Christian attackers. It shows the negative way Jews were portrayed during this time.

being devoted Christians, were willing to believe almost anything bad about their Jewish neighbors. One of the accusations that arose during the outbreak of the plague was the blood libel. Tuchman explained:

> Promoted by popular preachers, a mythology of blood grew in a mirror image of [Holy Communion], the Christian ritual of drinking [wine they believed became] the blood of the Saviour [Jesus Christ]. Jews were believed to kidnap and torture Christian children, whose blood they drank for a variety of sinister [evil] purposes ranging from sadism [love of hurting people] and sorcery to the need, as unnatural beings, for Christian blood to give them a human appearance.[34]

The reigning pope, Clement VI, tried to use simple logic to explain why Jews could not be guilty of causing the plague. He first pointed out that large numbers of Jews were dying of the disease. Why, he asked, would they want to kill many of their own kind? Moreover, numerous regions where no Jews lived were also struck by the plague, so there had to be some other cause. In an attempt to reduce violence, Pope Clement declared that no Christian should try "to capture, strike, wound, or kill any Jews."[35]

Unfortunately, anti-Semitism (prejudice against Jews) was so powerful in Europe that very few people listened to or obeyed the pope. Huge numbers of innocent Jews were massacred by angry mobs between 1348 and 1350. A surviving account by a German clergyman states that in the German town of Horw, all the Jews "were burnt in a pit."[36]

Sometimes Jews confessed to poisoning wells after being tortured. According to one document, a Jewish man was tortured in Switzerland and forced to confess that he carried "some prepared poison and venom in a thin, sewed leather-bag. [He planned to] distribute it among the wells, cisterns, and springs about Venice and the other places to which [Christians] go, in order to poison [them]."[37]

This forced confession was untrue. However, admissions such as this one gave townspeople across Europe another excuse to continue to persecute and kill Jews. The following account from the German town of Strasbourg told how the local Jews were burned alive in February 1349:

> [T]hey burnt the Jews on a wooden platform in their cemetery. There were about two thousand of them. Those who wanted to baptize themselves [as Christians] were spared. Many small children were taken out of the fire and baptized against the will of their fathers and mothers. And everything that was owed to the Jews was cancelled ... The [town] council, however, took the cash that the Jews possessed and divided it among the working-men proportionately ...

CLEMENS VI.
mouicens. creat. die
dit an. 10. mens. 7.
br. an. 1352. Vac.

Petrus Rogerius, Le=
7. Maij an. 1342. Se=
Obijt die 6. Decem
Sed. dies ii.

Pope Clement VI tried, unsuccessfully, to stop the persecution of European Jews.

After this wealth was divided among the artisans, some gave their share to the Cathedral or to the Church on the advice of their confessors.

[In] some towns they burnt the Jews after a trial, in others without a trial. In some cities the Jews themselves set fire to their houses.[38]

Modern scholars note this time period for being especially dark for European Jews. Despite being killed by the same virus as everyone else, their neighbors turned on them and blamed them for the Black Death.

Strange Times and Strange Behaviors

Thus, many cities across Europe attempted to fight the Black Death by murdering innocent Jews and other scapegoats in addition to imposing sanitation ordinances and restricting travel. When none of these acts were able to stop the epidemic, others appealed directly to God. However, when the plague continued, they soon came to feel that their prayers were being ignored.

Some of the most devout Christians joined groups of flagellants, a name that comes from the word flagellate, which means to punish by whipping. Groups of several hundred flagellants traveled from town to town and put on a kind of show. They would head directly to the local church or city center and beat themselves with a special whip that was called a scourge. According to an eyewitness, Heinrich of Herford, a scourge was "a kind of stick from which three tails with large knots hung down. Through the knots were thrust iron spikes ... With such scourges they lashed themselves on their ... bodies so that they became swollen and blue."[39]

These beatings were supposed to recreate the whippings Jesus received before his crucifixion. They believed that their suffering would convince God to be merciful and stop the spread of the Black Death.

However, this first session of whipping was only the beginning of a typical flagellant ceremony. Next, the worshippers sang dirges (sad songs), including one with these words: "Our journey's done in the holy name. / Christ Himself to Jerusalem came. / His cross He bore in His holy hand. / Help us, Savior of all the land." Sometimes they marched in circles, continuing to beat themselves and singing, "Come here for penance good and well, / thus we escape from burning hell!"[40]

Following this, it was common for the flagellants to lie down on the ground. Two of them then walked back and forth among them, beating them with scourges and reciting, "By Mary's honor free from stain, / arise and do not sin again."[41] Obeying this order, the men on the ground stood up and began beating themselves again. The final step of their demonstration was to

Flagellants often walked ceremoniously into a city center before they began their ritual beating.

listen as one of the masters gave what was known as the Flagellants' Sermon. The flagellants claimed that these sermons were the words of an angel sent by God. They warned that everyone in Europe was a sinner, and the only way to stop the Black Death was to return to God's ways.

At first, many of the townsfolk who watched this strange public display admired the dedication of the flagellants. They donated money or allowed the

flagellants to stay in their homes. The most extreme believers even joined the movement and traveled across the countryside. Over time, however, people grew tired of the self-torturers. Because the flagellants claimed that their sacrifices would prevent the plague, it looked bad when large numbers of them caught the disease and died. They were shown to be just as vulnerable to the Black Death as anyone else.

Moreover, the flagellants had become a threat to the central Catholic Church. In October 1349, Pope Clement issued a statement that said the flagellants were not supported by

God or the Church. Influential local churchmen also made similar speeches. Town mayors and councils began denying the groups entrance to their cities. As a result of these efforts, the wandering groups steadily disbanded. By the mid-1350s, a writer noted that a majority of the flagellants had disappeared, "vanishing as suddenly as they had come, like night phantoms or mocking ghosts."[42]

Devastation and Destruction in Europe

Flagellants, priests, town leaders, and nobles were unable to stop or even slow down the Black Death. It continued killing people and animals and disrupting societies and nations. The number of quick and painful deaths did not start to decrease until the early 1350s. Finally, the epidemic had run its course. Modern estimates claim that roughly 75 million people died from this single disease. The world's population was just 500 million people at that time. That amounts to a staggering 15 percent of the human race.

There is no doubt that Europe suffered particularly hard losses. Pope Clement's agents and French writer Jean Froissart estimated that one-third

PAINFUL RHYMES

The flagellants sang many unique songs during their public whippings, all of which were meant to praise God and ask for mercy at the same time. One song's lyrics were as follows:

> [W]hoe'er to save his soul is fain [whoever wants to save their soul],
> Must pay and render back again.
> His safety so shall he consult:
> Help us, good Lord, to this result …
> Lord, with loud voice we answer thee,
> Accept our service in return,
> And save us lest in hell we burn …
> Ply [apply] well the scourge for Jesus' sake,
> And God through Christ your sins shall take.
> For love of God abandon sin
> To mend your vicious lives begin,
> So shall we his mercy win.[1]

1. Quoted in J.F.C. Hecker, *The Epidemics of the Middle Ages, vol. 1.* Philadelphia, PA: Haswell, Barrington & Haswell, 1837, p. 62.

of the continent's inhabitants were wiped out. Some modern researchers agree with this figure, while others estimate that it was closer to one-half. Otto Friedrich, a leading expert on the plague, summed up Europe's wreckage:

The chronicles of the fourteenth century [present] an image of deserted cottages falling in ruins and untilled wheat fields reverting to wilderness. Thousands of villages all across the face of Europe did simply disappear. The buried remnants are faintly visible in aerial photographs, spectral outlines of a vanished people, and in England alone more than two thousand such ruins have been recorded. The Germans even have a word, Dorfwustungen, for the process of villages turning into wilderness. The depopulation of the cities was no less remarkable. [In fact], virtually no city anywhere regained its population of [the year] 1300 in less than two centuries.[43]

CHAPTER THREE

BLACK DEATH FACTS

Because the Black Death is such a widely-known epidemic, it can be hard to separate what is true from what is just a myth. Three main facts are generally agreed on about the plague's outbreak in Europe in the 1300s. First, many people were dying every day from a frightening disease. Second, although people had different ideas about the cause of the plague, nobody could say with certainty that they knew what was causing the disease to spread. Third, because of this confusion about the plague's cause, doctors were unable to control the spread of the disease—and they definitely could not cure it.

Doctors did not have the medical knowledge to explain the deadly events in Europe during the 1300s, but today, scientists are able explain the plague and set the facts straight. This is mainly because there were many scientific advances beginning in the 1600s and 1700s that led scientists to learn much more about the world around them. In addition to other discoveries, scientists introduced the germ theory in the 1800s. This theory quickly developed after the discovery of tiny microbes, or germs, which were able to invade the body, unknown to the host, and cause a number of diseases.

This groundbreaking theory triggered much research into various diseases, including the one that caused the Black Death. Most medical researchers and historians agree that the main cause of this terrifying epidemic was bubonic plague. In his book *The Black Death and the Transformation of the West*, scholar David Herlihy provided a brief explanation of the breakthrough research of the 1890s:

> *Most notably in 1894, in China, the plague emerged from the inland provinces [and attacked] the port city of*

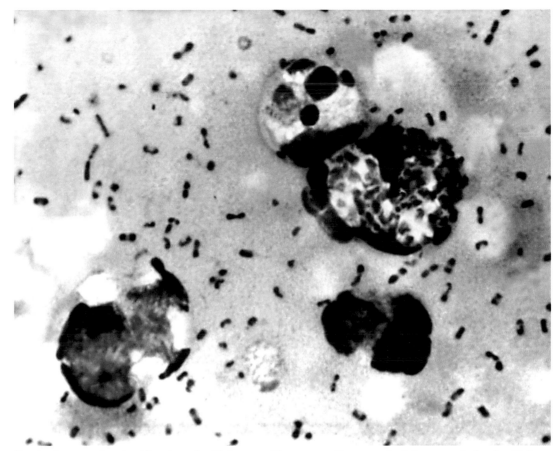

Bacteria were fascinating to scientists once they were discovered. Advances led scientists to learn about Yersinia pestis, *the bacteria that caused the plague, which is shown above.*

Hong Kong ... A Swiss microbiologist named Alexandre Yersin ... was then serving in the French colonial service in Indo-China. He hurried to Hong Kong and set up a laboratory there, in hopes of containing the disease before it struck southeast Asia. In 1894 he isolated the bacillus [plague germ] and went on to develop a serum for the treatment of plague. The disease is consequently called ... Yersinia pestis, *after Alexandre Yersin.*[44]

As time went on, researchers were able to better understand how bubonic plague appears, reproduces, and spreads. This allowed scientists and doctors to find ways for people to avoid catching the disease. Even when a person does catch it, medical authorities can keep it from spreading and becoming an epidemic. In addition, learning the real facts about the plague has helped modern society answer many questions about the events of the 1300s. It is now clear, for example, why medieval doctors' treatments were ineffective and why some people contracted the disease while others did not.

Timing Is Everything

One of the first things researchers noticed about bubonic plague, or the bacterium named *Yersinia pestis*, is that it naturally affects rats and other rodents—not humans. Outbreaks in human populations, experts say, are much less common than those in animal populations. Scientists have found that at any given time, a few rodents or other small creatures in a handful of remote wilderness areas are carrying the disease. These small groups of animals make up what medical experts call a disease reservoir. Most of the time, the animals in disease reservoirs have too few bacteria in their systems to kill them or to cause the illness to spread. In other words, the plague sleeps in these carriers. For a few years, decades, or in some cases centuries, it remains trapped and dormant in its reservoir, as if waiting for the perfect moment to escape.

Evidence shows that, on occasion, the plague germs living in one or more wild animals become numerous enough to begin spreading from one animal to another. Most often, it is because of the fleas that live in many animals' fur.

AN EARLY THEORY

Contrary to popular opinion, not all medieval doctors were totally unaware of what causes most diseases. Two brilliant 14th-century Islamic scholars, Ibn Khatima and Ibn al-Khatib, proposed an early theory of what they called "infection." Although not precisely the germ theory introduced in the 19th century by European scientists, this early version was partially correct and still far ahead of its time:

> To those who say, "How can we admit the possibility of infection while the religious law denies it?" we reply that the existence of contagion is established by experience, investigation, the evidence of the senses and trustworthy reports. These facts constitute a sound argument. The fact of infection becomes clear to the investigator who notices how he who establishes contact with the afflicted [sick person] gets the disease, whereas he who is not in contact remains safe, and how transmission is effected through garments, vessels and earrings.[1]

1. Quoted in Philip K. Hitti, *History of The Arabs*. Hong Kong, SAR: Macmillan, 1979, p. 576.

A common kind of flea is *Xenopsylla cheopis*, which is also called the rat flea. This flea consumes its host's blood, which contains plague bacteria. The germs have little or no effect on fleas, but they do manage to spread when a carrier flea lands on and bites an un-infected animal. The process rapidly repeats itself, and the result can be an epidemic among wild creatures.

When these infected animals remain isolated from human civilization, the disease will run its course and eventually begin to subside. However, when the infected animals come into contact with humans, a very different scenario takes place. As scholar James C. Giblin explained, this is how bubonic plague in the 1300s most likely spread from rodents in remote sections of central Asia to people:

Although it was only an eighth of an inch long, the rat flea was a tough, adaptable creature. It depended for nourishment on the blood of its host, which it obtained through a dagger-like snout that could pierce the rat's skin. And in its stomach the flea often carried thousands of the deadly bacteria that caused the bubonic plague ... A black rat could tolerate a moderate amount of [the germs] without showing ill effects. But sometimes the flea contained so many bacteria that they invaded the rat's lungs or nervous system when the flea injected its snout. Then the rat died a swift and horrible death, and the flea had to find a new host.

Aiding the tiny flea in its search were its powerful legs, which could jump more than 150 times the creature's length. In most instances the flea landed on another black rat ... [But] if most of the rats in the vicinity were already dead or dying from the plague, the flea might leap to a human being [nearby] instead.[45]

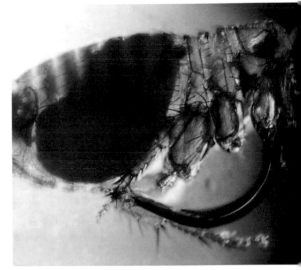

Rat fleas are most likely to blame for the spread of the bubonic plague bacteria. This flea is shown with its stomach full of blood.

Symptoms of Infection

After making the fateful jump to a person, the hungry flea immediately bit its new host. In the 1300s, this was probably a hunter or a trader who perhaps felt a slight pinch. They did not realize that this innocent bite signaled the initial attack of an invisible but deadly invasion force. During the feeding process, the insect transferred some plague germs into the bite wound. The bacteria worked its way into the person's lymph nodes. (These organs contain cells that help the body's immune system fight foreign invaders, including germs.)

The *Yersinia pestis* germs found the lymph nodes to be ideal places to multiply. Soon, they created colonies that increased in size, and within three to eight days, the germs formed lumps the size of eggs or larger. These lumps are the buboes that numerous medieval writers mentioned when describing the classic symptoms of the Black Death. Most often, the buboes appeared in the underarms or the groin.

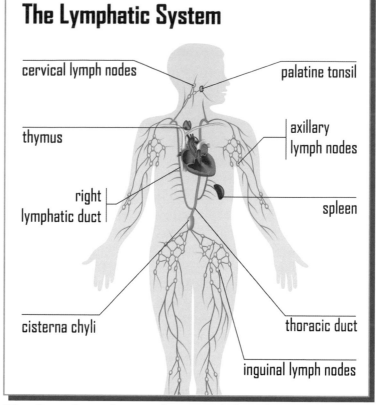

The Lymphatic System

cervical lymph nodes

palatine tonsil

thymus

axillary lymph nodes

right lymphatic duct

spleen

cisterna chyli

thoracic duct

inguinal lymph nodes

The plague bacteria entered a person's lymphatic system and traveled to the bloodstream from there. In this way, a person's body was quickly infested with bubonic plague.

After several more days had passed, the germs reached the victim's bloodstream. The bloodstream transported the germs to the vital organs, including the lungs and spleen. Soon, dark spots appeared on the skin, and in many cases, blood oozed from the skin as well. Next, Giblin wrote, "the nervous system started to collapse, causing dreadful pain [in the limbs] and bizarre movements of the arms and legs. Then,

as death neared, the mouth gaped open and the skin blackened from internal bleeding."[46]

The death of the victim was not the end of the process, however. The next phase in the lethal cycle began after death. Just as the infected fleas had earlier jumped off their dead rat hosts, the fleas now left behind the dead human ones. Still full of *Yersinia pestis*, the fleas searched for, and sometimes found, a new human host. From hunters and traders to sailors, city dwellers, farmers, and others, the germs ravaged one host after another.

Most modern experts agree that the Black Death followed this general scenario. The main evidence used to support this view is that the medieval writers described symptoms identical or at least very similar to those seen in modern cases of plague. In fact, several of these classic symptoms were mentioned by Italian eyewitness Michael of Piazza in his description of the Black Death's widespread outbreak in the mid-1300s. He wrote,

> Here not only the "burn blisters" appeared, but there developed gland boils on the groin, the thighs, the arms, or on the neck. At first these were of the size of a hazel nut, and developed accompanied by violent shivering fits, which soon rendered those attacked so weak that they could not stand up, but were forced to lie in their beds consumed by violent fever. Soon the boils grew to the size of a walnut, then to that of a hen's egg or a goose's egg, and they were exceedingly painful, and irritated the body, causing the sufferer to vomit blood. The sickness lasted three days, and on the fourth, at the latest, the patient succumbed. As soon as anyone in Catania [a town in Sicily] was seized with a headache and shivering, he knew that he was bound to pass away within the specified time.[47]

The Trail of Evidence

These medieval descriptions of the Black Death have long been interesting to epidemiologists. Epidemiologists track down and study clues to the various ways that germs spread disease. For them, it was not enough to know how the plague bacteria made it out of an animal reservoir in central Asia and infected humans. It is obvious that those infected people proceeded to carry the deadly germs to one or more nearby towns. Epidemiologists wanted to know much more. They wanted to be able to trace, as best as they could, the course of the Black Death as it made its way through the Middle East and Europe. Piecing together this chain of evidence would help modern scientists better understand this killer disease and thereby keep it from causing a new wave of Black Death.

Fortunately for medical researchers, historians had already started piecing together the important string of events that caused the spread of the Black Death. That chain begins in Kaffa, the Crimean port city that was attacked by the Mongols early in 1346. The residents of Kaffa were naturally concerned when the enemy started lobbing diseased corpses over the city's walls. They were aware that these bodies were causing them to come down with a terrible sickness, but they had no idea how the disease was spreading among them. They had no clue that the disease they were experiencing followed unique paths of infection.

Medical expert Alfred J. Bollet explained,

The corpses catapulted over the walls of Kaffa may not have been carrying competent plague [carriers]. Rats were not catapulted, but the city must have had its own supply [of rats]. The cadavers [dead bodies] may still have had infected fleas on them (either human or rat fleas, or both) and could thus have spread the disease inside the besieged city, or the infection could have been spread by [flea-infested] rats migrating into and out of the city despite the siege.[48]

There were two key carriers that spread the Black Death beyond Kaffa: rats and people on whom one or more fleas had made a temporary home. Although it was the fleas that carried the actual plague germs, they could not have made it out of the city and onto ships without rats and humans to carry them.

Of these two carriers, the rats were by far the most numerous and ultimately

This illustration shows what the Mongolian siege of Kaffa might have looked like.

In medieval Europe, rats could be found living alongside humans in both urban and rural areas.

lethal. Indeed, a major reason that the disease was able to spread so quickly from one city or country to another was that no one suspected that rats were carrying the disease. After all, they were practically everywhere. Rats and other rodents scrounged for food in farmers' fields and barns, grain supplies, houses, shops, ships, and elsewhere. People had accepted them as pesky but ever-present nuisances. They never suspected that the rats were helping the transmission of the Black Death from place to place.

No one took notice as a few infected rats or some carrying infected fleas crawled from docks onto ships. The ships carried these live disease-carriers from Kaffa to ports near and far. Harbormasters in a city that had not yet encountered the disease often ordered the crews and passengers of newly arrived ships to stay onboard. This is what happened when Genoese ships from the East reached the southern Italian port of Messina. However, the strategy of keeping potentially infected people from leaving the ships did not prevent the spread of the plague. The harbormasters "had no way of knowing," Giblin pointed out, "that the actual carriers of the disease had already

SCARED DOCTORS

Many medieval doctors died of the bubonic plague during the Black Death. The fact that they had no knowledge or ability to stop the epidemic was a tremendous embarrassment to those who managed to survive. A distinguished French physician of that time, Gui de Chauliac, wrote,

> The plague [was] shameful for the physicians, who could give no help at all, especially as, out of fear of infection, they hesitated to visit the sick. Even if they did, they achieved nothing, and earned no fees, for all those who caught the plague died, except for a few towards the end of the epidemic who had escaped after the buboes had ripened.[1]

1. Quoted in Edouard Nicaise, ed., *La Grande Chirurgie*. Paris, France: Alcan, 1890, p. 171.

left the ships. Under cover of night, when no one could see them, they [the infected rats] had scurried down the ropes that tied the ships to the dock and vanished into [the city]."[49]

Three Diseases in One

Once the rats carrying the infected fleas entered Messina and other port cities, the next step in the plague's assault on Europe took place. Some fleas hopped off the rats and found human hosts. Many of those new hosts caught the plague. When those victims died, the fleas jumped to either other humans or animals and spread the contagion in all directions.

For the people infected with the plague, there were three possible forms for the disease to take. The most common was the passage of *Yersinia*

pestis from the lymph nodes to the major organs of the body, producing the symptoms described previously. Medical experts generally refer to this form of the illness, which was fatal in 50 to 60 percent of cases, as bubonic.

In a minority of cases, however, the disease could take two other forms. The first is called pneumonic plague, because it involves a rare kind of pneumonia. Sometimes, when an infected person is exposed to a sudden and sharp drop in temperature, the germs can move into the lungs. The victim rapidly develops a severe cough and begins spitting up bloody mucus. Because the mucus contains plague microbes, it can infect other people or animals directly when it flies into the air or lands on nearby objects. It is therefore extremely contagious and

Rats carrying fleas and plague bacteria are responsible for all three types of the disease.

dangerous. Almost every case of pneumonic plague was fatal.

The third and rarest form of the disease, septicemic plague, occurs when the bacteria enter the bloodstream immediately and in huge numbers. As the germs move through the body, they multiply quickly. Within hours they infect all areas of the body, resulting in certain death in less than one day. British scholar Philip Ziegler wrote about septicemic plague:

> The victim is dead long before buboes have had time to form. It is in this form of plague that Pulex irritans, *the man-borne flea, has a chance to operate. So rich in bacilli [plague germs] is the blood of a sick man that the flea can easily infect itself and carry on the disease to a new prey without the need of a rat to provide fresh sources of infection. [Septicemic] plague must have been the rarest of the three interwoven diseases which composed the Black Death but it was certainly as lethal as its pneumonic cousin and it introduced yet another means by which the plague could settle itself in a new area and spread hungrily among the inhabitants.*[50]

Not-So-Random Killing

It is important to note that some people in the 1300s, as well as in outbreaks of the plague in later eras, were exposed to the disease but did not contract it. The Black Death seemed to kill randomly. Often it wiped out entire families or neighborhoods and villages. In other instances, though people did not contract the plague despite being in close contact with the infected.

Experts point to a number of reasons for this. First, the most frequent form, bubonic plague, was rarely contagious person-to-person. The main carrier was infected fleas, so a person's chances of getting sick depended on their exposure to the fleas, not the infected human. Therefore, the disease spread more easily in areas with poor sanitation, where more diseased fleas and rats were likely to gather. In areas where homes and streets were cleaner, more people escaped infection. Moreover, because the deadly fleas often inhabited animal fur, people who had minimal contact with animals were less likely to get sick.

An even more important factor affecting the plague's ability to spread was personal immunity. As historian Robert S. Gottfried pointed out, "in the Middle Ages, active immunity was particularly important in determining the extent and intensity of an epidemic."[51] Modern medical researchers have found that, for a variety of reasons, some people have stronger immune systems than others. Thus, a person with strong immunity had a good chance of fighting off the infection, especially if their exposure was relatively light. As a result of these factors and others, some people who were directly exposed to others suffering from the Black Death did not catch it.

A Plan of Action

If medieval physicians had known about any of these factors, or the fact that the plague was caused by germ-infested fleas, they might have been able to slow or prevent the disease's

The plague spread so quickly that people tried anything they could think of to stop it. Their methods were largely unsuccessful. In this painting, they are asking God for help.

spread. However, the sad fact is that they were completely unaware of the plague's causes and modes of transmission. Because modern doctors and scientists have figured out these facts,

they can explain why their medieval counterparts failed to treat the illness.

Doctors working in the 1300s frequently used the cures and treatments suggested by the ancient Greek

GALEN, AN ADMIRED PHYSICIAN

Galen was one of the most admired ancient physicians in medieval times. He was born in the Greek city of Pergamum in AD 129 and grew up to be a brilliant scholar and the leading medical practitioner in the Roman Empire. He studied and promoted the ideas of well-known doctors who came before him, especially Hippocrates, the fifth-century BC Greek scholar who was later called the father of medicine. Like Hippocrates, Galen argued that disease is a natural phenomenon rather than a divine punishment. He performed numerous experiments, including the dissection of pigs, dogs, and other animals.

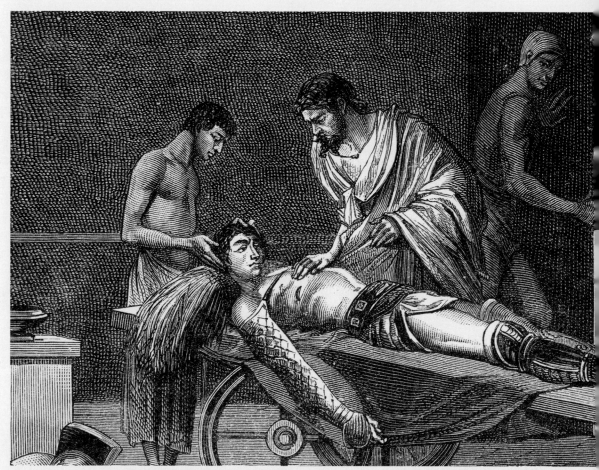

Galen's medical texts and drawings were used for many years because he was known as a great physician. In this illustration, he is shown treating a wounded gladiator.

In addition, he wrote hundreds of medical essays, of which about 150 complete or partial texts still survive. It was these writings, along with Galen's reputation as the supreme Greco-Roman medical expert, which made him incredibly popular among doctors and other educated people in the Middle Ages. It took until the early 17th century for medical science to significantly surpass Galen's ancient medical achievements.

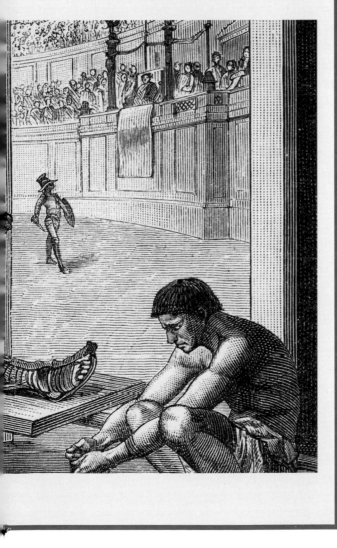

physician and medical researcher named Galen. He was important in his own day because he did extensive medical research when most other physicians did not. However, the doctors in later ages who followed his teachings did little or no research of their own. They blindly accepted his claims that illness resulted from factors such as a person's personality traits, the temperature or "purity" of the air, and eating or drinking too much. Accordingly, doctors faced with the Black Death told their patients they could avoid the disease by hanging fragrant flowers or herbs throughout their homes.

Unfortunately for patients who were already sick with plague, doctors often prescribed bloodletting as a remedy. This consisted of opening one or more veins, especially those located near buboes, and allowing "tainted" blood to drain out into a pan. Needless to say, this only made the patient weaker. Opening and draining the buboes was also common, though this was ineffective because bacteria still remained inside and continued to multiply.

There were numerous approaches to curing the plague tried by doctors. Almost none of these actually did anything to help. Many tried applying various substances to the buboes, including a widely popular mixture of tree resin, ground lily roots, and human excrement. Other patients were told to drink crushed emeralds mixed with water, a toxic brew that was more likely to kill the patient than the plague germs. Finally, when all else failed, people turned to prayer.

In modern times, doctors and other medical professionals do not have to deal with the plague very often. However, when they do, they possess treatments that are effective in the vast majority of cases. The standard treatment for the plague is to isolate the victim and then administer a strong antibiotic to kill the bacteria.

At first, this may seem like a simple solution to a major problem. However, it is important to remember that it took thousands of researchers working diligently over the course of more than 100 years to accumulate enough scientific information to make this solution a reality. Everyone alive today can consider themselves fortunate that they were born after, rather than before, the facts about the plague and other terrible diseases came to light.

CHAPTER FOUR

ECONOMIC EFFECTS OF THE PLAGUE

When people discuss the Black Death that hit Europe in the 1300s, they frequently focus on the high death toll. The number of deaths was so overwhelming that it is natural to discuss it. Equally important, however, is that those lucky enough to survive were now left with a very different world. There is a tendency to assume that life for most people just went back to normal after the plague had subsided. For example, people who were poor peasants before the plague remained poor peasants afterwards. The reality is actually far different from that assumption.

The destruction caused by the plague in Europe changed most aspects of peoples' lives. Social classes and customs, literature, the arts, and religion were all impacted, and some things changed

forever. However, the greatest changes, both immediate and long-term, were economic. The price of food and other important goods and services, occupations, relations between management and workers, and the very structure of the economy were altered in a major way. These effects, as well as others, changed the way that many people, especially the poor and oppressed, saw the society in which they lived. The economic changes were so serious that some scholars rank them among the factors that brought about the decline of medieval times and the rise of early modern Europe.

The Medieval Manorial System

The biggest single economic change after the Black Death was the decline of the medieval manorial system. This system was based on the manor, which was a large house and the surrounding lands owned by a wealthy noble. The people who worked on a typical manor were called peasants and owed loyalty to the noble who owned it. Those below his social class generally referred to that owner as "my lord." The lord gave peasants land, a place to live, and protection. In exchange, the peasants labored for him, typically for life. They either worked in the fields, planting and harvesting crops, or did some other form of work.

The vast majority of these laborers were serfs: poor people who were generally attached to the estate on which they lived and worked. Though they were free to leave and look for work somewhere else, if they did so, they no longer had a reliable way to feed their families. Leaving the manor also meant losing the legal and military protection the lord of the manor had provided for them. Afraid that they might not be able to find an equally stable situation elsewhere, most stayed put. They, their children, and their grandchildren remained serfs, providing the cheap labor that made the manorial system possible.

Serfs were the backbone of the manorial system. When millions of those workers suddenly died, that system collapsed. The Black Death killed so many people that entire sections of Europe rapidly depopulated. Nearly every manor across Europe suffered terrible losses. A French poet who lived through the disaster described the effects of depopulation on the large agricultural estates:

> For many have certainly
> Heard it commonly said
> How in one thousand three hun-
> dred and forty-nine [the year 1349]
> Out of one hundred there remained
>   but nine [workers on a manor]
> Thus it happened that for lack
>   of people
> Many a splendid farm was
>   left untilled
> No one plowed the fields
> Bound the cereals [grains] and took
>   in the grapes.[52]

With so much death, many of the nobles who owned manors with extensive agricultural land no longer had enough cheap laborers. They were forced into a difficult position: They could not turn profits without major changes to their manor. From 1347 to 1353, English lords saw a 20 percent decrease in profits. At the same time, the surviving peasants inhabiting those manors decided to put an added burden on the owners. Many of these serfs realized they suddenly had some bargaining power and demanded a better financial arrangement. The biggest issue for these serfs was an increase in pay.

As a result of these combined factors, the nobles who had long run the manorial system found

The manorial system was based on peasants laboring for their lords, as shown here. Because of the Black Death, this system crumbled.

themselves in an economic crisis. According to historian Robert S. Gottfried,

The value of agricultural products began to fall, and it stayed low relative to that of industrial goods until the sixteenth century; at the same time, depopulation made agricultural workers scarce and, thus, much more valuable. Wages rose rapidly … [At] Cuxham Manor in England, a plowman who was paid 2 shillings a week in 1347 received 7 shillings in 1349, and 10 shillings [by] 1350. The result was a dramatic rise in standards of living for those in the lower [social classes]. Day laborers not only received higher wages, but asked for and got lunches of meat pies and golden ale [beer].[53]

The Commoners' Demands

Modern scholars and historians base their findings on surviving documents from the era of the Black Death. Several of these writings describe an upside-down world in which traditional values and prices abruptly underwent massive change. The members of the upper classes found it inappropriate, and even disgraceful, that poorer people began taking advantage of the nobility. Suddenly, these economic demands were coming not only from agricultural laborers, but also commoners in a wide range of jobs in the towns and cities. They wanted higher pay and more benefits, just like their serf counterparts. Furthermore, they were now enjoying goods, services, and customs normally reserved for the wealthy and

CITIES DESTROYED

The major economic cost of the Black Death was not restricted to Europe. The extensive Islamic regions of the Middle East and North Africa were also devastated. According to Ibn Khaldūn, a historian of the era,

Civilization both in the East and West was visited by a destructive plague, which devastated nations and caused populations to vanish. It swallowed up many of the good things of civilization and wiped them out … Cities and buildings were laid waste, roads and way signs were obliterated, settlements and mansions became empty, and dynasties [family lines of rulers] grew weak. The entire inhabited world changed … It was as if the voice of existence in the world had called out for oblivion and restriction and the world responded to its call. God inherits the earth and whoever is upon it.[1]

1. Quoted in Michael Dols, *The Black Death in the Middle East*. Princeton, NJ: Princeton University Press, 1977, p. 67.

social elite. In 1363, Italian chronicler Matteo Villani reported,

> The common folk, both men and women ... would no longer labour at their accustomed trades, but demanded the dearest and most delicate [fine] foods for their sustenance; and they married at their will, while children and common women clad themselves in all the fair and costly garments of the [upper-class] ladies dead by that horrible death [the plague]. Thus, almost the whole city [Florence], without any restraint whatsoever, rushed into disorderliness of life ... Men dreamed of wealth and abundance in garments and in all other things ... [and] the work of all trades and crafts rose in disorderly fashion beyond the double.[54]

Villani also gave the following examples of "arrogant" members of the lower classes who demanded and got better wages and benefits:

> Serving girls and unskilled women with no experience in service and stable boys want at least 12 florins per year, and the most arrogant among them 18 or 24 florins per year, and so also nurses and minor artisans working with their hands want three times [the] usual pay, and laborers on the land all want oxen and all seed, and want to work the best lands, and to abandon all other [lands and allow nature to reclaim them].[55]

It was not only the traditionally poor classes that took advantage of the widespread death. Skilled professionals, especially doctors, suffered terrible losses during the plague. Because these professionals had to be in close contact with the plague's victims, very few were willing to step up to replace them. The replacements were able to charge premium prices for their services, simply because they were the only ones who would do them. The clergy was also hit particularly hard:

> There was so great scarcity and rarity of priests that parish churches remained altogether unserved ... [and] many chaplains and hired parish priests would not serve without excessive pay. The Bishop of Rochester [intervened and] commanded these [priests] to serve at the same salaries [as before], under pain of suspension.[56]

Preserving Class Distinctions

The significant increase in salaries was not the only example of rising prices in the years following the Black Death. Because so many people, including artisans and other skilled workers, had died during the epidemic, very few people were left to produce everyday goods. These included food, wine, fabrics, clothing, linens, pottery, metal utensils and weapons, building materials, and more. The production of fewer goods made those goods more valuable. This contributed to a general rise in the prices of goods and services throughout society, which is known as inflation. This inflation "persisted until the last decades of the fourteenth century," historian David Herlihy wrote. This meant "that under the shock of [the] plague, production in town and countryside had fallen even more rapidly than the population."[57]

Most of the nobles and other wealthy people could afford to pay the higher prices, of course, although they were certainly unhappy about it. Before the plague, there was no way that most members of the lower classes could afford to pay the inflated prices. However, because of the plague, large numbers of these workers had demanded and were now making more money. As Villani pointed out, many people who were not used to luxuries now ate fine foods and wore expensive garments.

The peasants undoubtedly appreciated this change in lifestyle. However,

PRIESTS INFLATE FEES

In the wake of the Black Death there was widespread suffering and a greatly increased need for spiritual aid for commoners who had survived the epidemic. A number of priests and other churchmen took advantage of the situation by charging higher fees than normal. In November 1378 the archbishop of Canterbury wrote a letter to the bishop of London, complaining that

[Many priests in Canterbury] have been so infected with the sin of greed that, not satisfied with reasonable wages, they hire themselves out for vastly inflated salaries. And these same greedy and pleasure-seeking priests vomit out the enormous salaries with which they are stuffed.[1]

Since there were so few priests at this time, they were able to demand higher pay. The Bishop of Rochester put an end to this practice.

1. Quoted in Rosemary Horrox, ed., *The Black Death. Manchester*, UK: Manchester University Press, 1994, p. 311.

the upper classes, who were used to being the only people who could enjoy luxury, hated this trend. They were angry to see people they viewed as inferiors enjoying access to fine goods. "Conspicuous consumption [showing off wealth] by the humble threatened to erase the visible marks of social distinctions and to undermine the social order,"[58] one expert remarked.

Hoping to keep the class system clearly divided, the nobles who ran the governments across Europe passed hundreds of laws regulating how people could spend money in the century following the Black Death. These were restrictions designed to limit displays of wealth. For instance, women were forbidden to wear dresses that did not conform to a certain style, and only certain types of food and drink could be served at weddings.

These laws were written so that they applied to members of the lower classes but not to aristocratic people. The obvious goal was that these laws would reinforce the boundaries between the social classes. Unfortunately for the upper classes, they did not work. The higher living standards of many commoners in the post-plague years remained a fact of life for the remainder of the medieval era.

Trouble Among the People

In desperation, a few national rulers and town governments tried to keep the lower social groups in their place by more obvious and forceful means.

Access to fine clothing was restricted among lower-class citizens. A dress such as the one seen here would have been reserved for the nobility.

Some rules forbade peasants from leaving the manors on which they had been raised. Others kept commoners who worked in shops and other businesses from switching jobs. Still others placed limits on how much commoners could earn in various jobs and professions. As scholar Philip Ziegler explained, the object of these rules

> was to pin wages and prices as closely as possible to a pre-plague figure and thus to check the inflation that [began during the Black Death]. The Government realized that this could never be achieved as long as labourers were free to move from one employer to another in search of higher wages and so long as employers were free to woo away laborers from their neighbors with [tempting] offers. By restricting the right of an employee to leave his place of work, by compelling him to accept work when it was offered to him, by forbidding the employer to offer wages greater than those paid three years before ... [and] by fixing the prices which butchers, bakers, and fishmongers could charge their customers, they hoped to recreate the conditions that pertained [existed] before the plague and maintain them for ever.[59]

Any citizen who ignored these oppressive rules was taxed or fined, and some who refused to pay the fines were arrested. Such extreme measures ended up affecting everyone except society's wealthiest members and, as such, were very unpopular. English chronicler Henry Knighton described the laws created in England during the late 14th century:

> The laborers were so lifted up and obstinate [stubborn] that they would not listen to the king's [new rules] ... And when it was known to the king that they had not observed his command ... he levied heavy fines upon abbots, priors, knights, greater and lesser, and other great folk and small folk of the realm ... And afterwards the king had many labourers arrested, and sent them to prison; many withdrew themselves and went into the forests and woods; and those who were [caught] were heavily fined. Their ringleaders were made to swear that they would not take daily wages beyond the ancient custom, and then were freed from prison. And in like manner was done with the other craftsmen in the boroughs and villages.[60]

These attempts to regulate wages and maintain the old social order only made peasants and other commoners angry. The result was a series of uprisings by workers that foreshadowed the larger anti-aristocratic revolutions that would rock Europe in the 1700s and 1800s. Probably the best-known example in the 14th century occurred in France in 1358. Because French peasants were often called "Jacques," it was called the Jacquerie. The French chronicler Jean Froissart recorded the following:

> [A large number of enraged peasants] gathered together without any other counsel [leaders], and without

vant messire berte
ray de dauegun
fut arue en lost.
les francois en fu

lenesgue et les citoiens se tourne
rent francois et rendirent la ate
au duc de berry gui y entra auec
luy le duc de bourbon messire

The peasants in France protested their treatment and fought for more freedom during their uprising in 1358.

any armour [except for] staves and knives, and so went to the house of a knight dwelling thereby, and [broke] up his house and slew the knight and the lady and all his children great and small and [burned] his house. And they then went to another castle, and took the knight thereof and bound him fast to a stake, and then … slew the lady and his daughter and all his other children, and then slew the knight by great torment and burnt and beat down the castle. And so they did to divers [many] other castles and good houses; and they multiplied so that they were a six thousand [rebels], and ever as they went forward they increased [in number] … so that every gentleman fled from them and took their wives and children with them … and left their house void and their goods therein. These mischievous people thus assembled without captain … robbed, [burned], and slew all gentlemen that they could lay hands on.[61]

These violent acts were an expression of the anger that had been building up in peasants for generations. After the plague, they had finally gotten a taste of a better life, and just like the nobles, they were unwilling to give it up without a fight. These feelings were not unique to the French. A similarly large peasant revolt occurred in England in 1381. There, King Richard II felt so threatened that he came to a legal agreement with the peasants,

PEASANT REBELLIONS

England's peasant revolt in 1381 was one of the largest rebellions of the post-plague period. Tens of thousands of people marched to London and tried to see King Richard II. A local chronicler recalled,

[T]hey directed their way to the Tower [of London] where the king was surrounded by a great throng [group] of knights, esquires, and others [attempting to protect him] … They [the peasants] complained that they had been seriously oppressed by many hardships and that their condition of servitude was unbearable, and that they neither could nor would endure it longer. The king, for the sake of peace, and on account of the violence of the times, yielding to their petition, granted them a charter [agreement] … to the effect that all men in the kingdom … should be free and of free condition.[1]

1. Quoted in Leon Bernard and Theodore B. Hodges, eds., *Readings in European History*. New York, NY: Macmillan, 1958, pp. 214–215.

granting them a number of rights and freedoms they had never before possessed. Although the king and his nobles did not end up honoring the agreement, England's lower classes

The peasant revolt of 1381, shown here, was also called Wat Tyler's Rebellion, named after one of the leaders of the uprising.

did gain some rights by compromising with King Richard. The government had to reduce taxes, and it was not permitted to pass any laws designed to keep the wages of ordinary laborers low. As a result of these substantial changes, England's traditional manorial system had vanished from most parts of the kingdom by the early 15th century.

Rich Landowners Start to Disappear

Historians note many economic effects of the plague's assault on Europe in the 14th century. One of the most interesting, but rarely mentioned, is a decrease in the number of rich landowners in some areas. This is not surprising considering that the main source of income on many large estates—peasant workers—had been seriously damaged by the Black Death. German scholar Friedrich Lutge summed up this trend, saying that as a result of the plague

> numerous peasant [land plots] were no longer occupied. Where they were occupied, the peasant was able to lessen his obligations [to the landowner] in many ways because he was in high demand. There was, moreover, a decline in the purchasing power of money ... Thus, [some of] the landlords became impoverished [and] the German knightly order was reduced to bankruptcy. [A suddenly poor noble often] took service, usually in a military or administrative capacity, with nobles who were still prosperous.[62]

This is another reminder of how the plague impacted every level of society. Not only did it kill both nobles and peasants, it also created an economic situation in which even some of the rich became poor, and some of the poor became rich.

CHAPTER FIVE

IMPACTS ON CULTURE

Although there were many economic effects of the Black Death on Europe, the economy was certainly not the only area affected by the plague. European culture was also significantly altered by the Black Death's deadly visit to the continent. Among the elements of life that were changed were learning, education, and literature; the arts and architecture; technology and science, including medicine; and religious faith and worship. As researcher Otto Friedrich wrote, the extermination of a large part of the human race affected people's outlook on life in profound ways, "and theories about the indirect effects of the Black Death touch on almost every aspect of life."[63] It was very difficult for Europeans to adjust to the major changes that had occurred in the 1300s.

Bad Behavior

Some of the most visible aspects of life that changed after the Black Death were communication skills, social manners, and general behaviors. According to many medieval writers, all of these changed for the worse. However, many of the worst examples were merely temporary. For instance, Boccaccio described various episodes of antisocial behavior that occurred at the height of the epidemic. These included brothers abandoning brothers, priests fleeing their churches, and parents neglecting their children. However, later observers pointed out that these shameful acts were part of the mass hysteria created by the immediate danger of horrible illness and death. As a result, these behaviors were widespread but only short-term. After the great outbreak of pestilence ran its course, such extreme reactions were less common.

Still, some of Boccaccio's peers wrote about other, more long-term negative changes in the following years. French monk and chronicler Jean de Venette said that a number of people displayed thoughtless and selfish behavior:

After [the] cessation [end] of the epidemic, pestilence, or plague, the men and women who survived married

Italian author Giovanni Boccaccio wrote about the hysterical behavior that people displayed during the Black Death years in Decameron.

each other [and had a new genera-tion of children] … But woe is me! the world was not changed for the bet-ter but for the worse by this renewal of population. For men were more [greedy] than before, even though they had far greater possessions. They were more covetous and disturbed each other more frequently with [law] suits, brawls, [and other] disputes … [Moreover] the enemies of the king of France and of the Church were stronger and wickeder than before and stirred up wars on sea and on land. Greater evils than before [spread] everywhere in the world.[64]

It is difficult to know how much of this description is based on changes that affected the entire continent and how much reflected mainly de Ven-ette's local experiences. Regardless, evidence does conclusively show that life did not go back to normal after the Black Death. As soon as fear of the plague begin to subside, several more outbreaks struck Europe in the second half of the century. Although smaller than the initial epidemic, these new threats discouraged many people and forced them to view life as uncertain and brutal. The possibility of dying from an unpreventable disease or facing an uncertain economic change made 14th-century and 15th-century Europe unstable. Before the Black Death, historian Robert Gottfried wrote, European literature and art "expressed a buoyant optimism [positivity]" about

life. In contrast, "after the Black Death, this was replaced by a pervasive pessimism [negativity]."[65]

Images of Death

Some experts speculate that people now had a more gruesome way of look-ing at the concepts of life and death. While everyone hoped for a long and successful life, most people now recog-nized how easily death could come to anyone. Because of the plague's peri-odic outbreaks and the huge amounts of death that came with them, the end of life was always right around the corner. The most common image of this new outlook was the macabre, a style that used skeletons and other im-ages of death as a centerpiece. Artists, sculptors, and writers all frequently used this new and popular style. Often, they showed or described one or more skeletons dancing, a frightening theme that is known as the danse macabre, or dance of death.

A widespread fascination with that chilling image spread all across Europe in the late 14th and early 15th centu-ries. As the noted Dutch historian Jo-han Huizinga explained, there was a "desire to invent a visible image of all that [represented] death." There was a particular attraction to "the cruder con-ceptions of death," which "impressed themselves continually on [people's] minds."[66] It was not just the loss of loved ones to the plague that motivated this obsession with dark and terrifying art. Rather, it was also the fear of one's

Skeletons were a common representation of death during the late 1300s, and images of them became popular.

own death, which they believed could come without warning.

The dance of death and other dark, pessimistic images were part of the larger view of a changed world. The general agreement in the post-plague years was that the traditional order of the universe had gone wrong. Some people argued that God had spread so much death because he was angry about human sins. However, many other people believed that the disaster was too big to be explained by God alone. There had to be some other factor, one that was perhaps beyond human understanding. According to historian Barbara W. Tuchman,

God's purposes were usually mysterious, but this scourge [curse] had been too terrible to be accepted without questioning. If a disaster of such magnitude, the most lethal ever known, was a mere wanton [random] act of God, or perhaps not God's work at all, then the absolutes of a fixed order were loosed from their moorings [foundations]. Minds that opened to admit these questions could never again be shut. Once people

"EVERYWHERE IS FEAR"

The onset of the Black Death inspired many Europeans to express their horror or sadness in writing. Some of these writings have come to be seen as pieces of literary art. One outstanding example is this letter from the Italian writer Petrarch to his brother, a monk:

> Alas! my beloved brother, what shall I say? How shall I begin? Whither [where] shall I turn? On all sides is sorrow; everywhere is fear. I [wish], my brother, that I had never been born, or, at least, had died before these times. How will posterity believe that there has been a time when without the lightnings of heaven or the fires of earth, without wars or other visible slaughter, not this or that part of the earth, but well-nigh [nearly] the whole globe, has remained without inhabitants. When has any such thing been even heard or seen; in what annals [histories] has it ever been read that houses were left vacant, cities deserted, the country neglected, the fields too small for the dead and a fearful and universal solitude over the whole earth?[1]

1. Quoted in "Petrarch on the Plague," Decameron Web, February 18, 2010. www.brown.edu/Departments/Italian_Studies/dweb/plague/perspectives/petrarca.php.

envisioned the possibility of change in a fixed order, the end of an age of submission came in sight; the turn to individual conscience lay ahead. To that extent, the Black Death may have been the unrecognized beginning of modern man.[67]

The Faithful Begin to Struggle

The way that most Europeans viewed death, God, and life in general had been permanently altered. One of the leading modern experts on the Black Death, Philip Ziegler, called it "a crisis of faith," arguing that

assumptions which had been taken for granted for centuries were now in question, the very framework of men's reasoning seemed to be breaking up. And though the Black Death was far from being the only cause, the anguish [pain] and disruption which it had inflicted made the greatest single contribution to the disintegration of an age.[68]

In Europe, the Roman Catholic Church was by far the largest spiritual institution during the Middle Ages. People looked to the Church and clergymen for guidance in every part of their lives. However, the Black Death

The Roman Catholic Church was greatly changed as a result of the plague. Some priests tried to help the sick, but many fled so they would not get sick themselves.

caused millions of devoted Christians to begin questioning their trust in priests, their relationship to God, and the pope himself.

Many Europeans in the 14th century were unsure of God's role in the spread of the plague because they believed God was invisible and did not communicate with people. On the other hand, members of the clergy were visible, and their behavior during the crisis was well known. Many priests and bishops died in the epidemic, so it was clear that

even a close relationship to God could not save someone from the disease. Some saw this as a strike against them. Many people also felt that the clergy had no ability to persuade God to stop the plague or spare the millions who died. Worst of all, however, was that many priests had simply abandoned their posts, leaving the people who put their faith in them to suffer and die, thinking that God abandoned them.

Despite many leaving their posts, nearly 50 percent of clergy across

Europe lost their lives to the plague. The central Church authorities needed to quickly replace as many of them as they could. Training programs in universities and on-the-job training were accelerated so that the new priests could start their jobs immediately. While these methods were effective in producing new clergy members, the priests were commonly regarded as being much worse than those who came before them. Some reports claimed that they were often not even literate, which was one of the greatest distinctions between common people and the clergy before the plague.

In addition, people felt that Pope Clement VI in Avignon, France, had not set a good example during the catastrophe. Rumors spread that instead of risking his life to help his followers, he went to extreme lengths to save only himself. This was mostly true. He enlisted the help of a prominent physician and shut himself up in privacy for months. There were rumors, which mostly turned out to be true, that he had servants build and maintain two massive fires in his room at all times. Interestingly, this actually did prevent Pope Clement from catching the plague, because rats and fleas did not like the extreme heat.

The Church's high place in society sustained a major blow. Following the outbreak of the Black Death, most Europeans continued to believe in God, and while some left the Catholic Church, many decided to stay. Those that remained now felt that priests were not necessarily the special individuals that most people had previously assumed they were. More shockingly, almost everyone now believed that the church had flaws. Although the church remained a powerful social institution, scholar James Giblin pointed out that

it never regained the complete authority it had enjoyed before the plague. Once people began to question the Church's actions, they kept on questioning them. This eventually led to attempts to reform the Roman Catholic Church and then, in the sixteenth century, to the establishment of the first Protestant churches.[69]

Many of the daily and yearly religious habits and traditions of Europeans began to change as the Church fell from its place of highest esteem. Before the plague, it was an everyday event for someone who felt troubled, worried, or lost to ask their local clergyman to pray for him or her. However, in the post-plague era, it became increasingly common for people to ask their loved ones to do so or to pray for themselves instead.

Interestingly, near the end of the Black Death in 1350, Europe witnessed a major increase in charitable giving. Hospitals, the poor, and others in need of public support benefited from the increase in good works by the faithful. In addition, large numbers of people left their normal activities and went on long, difficult pilgrimages to holy

Many people made long, difficult journeys to important holy places after the Black Death.

Christian shrines. Among the most popular were the church in Canterbury, England where Saint Thomas Becket had been murdered; the sites of Jesus's arrest, trial, and crucifixion in Jerusalem; Saint Peter's tomb in Rome; and Santiago de Compostela, a city in Spain where the shrine of Saint James is located.

Many scholars think that the increased religious offerings during this time period were believed to be a way to make peace with God. Those

who still believed in God hoped this would persuade God to not send any more destructive plagues to punish humanity.

New Scientific Knowledge

Science and knowledge in general were other important aspects of culture affected by the Black Death. The technological advances during the years after the plague are particularly important. As Gottfried pointed out, "there was a direct relationship between

technology and depopulation."[70] Before the plague began spreading in the mid-1300s, most unskilled labor was accomplished by hand or with the aid of some simple tools. However, when a large number of Europe's workers died in the epidemic, there were no longer enough hands to do all the work that needed to be done.

Solutions to this major problem needed to be found—and found fast. One obvious fix was to produce more tools that could make work easier. As a result, there were significant improvements to the most basic necessity for farming: the plow. Not only were these tools more widespread, but their improvement allowed farmers to accomplish more work in less time. However, simply improving old tools would not be enough. New kinds of devices were clearly needed, and thankfully, Gottfried claimed, "shortage" proved to be "the mother of medieval invention." The sudden removal of millions of workers from society "put a premium on new techniques that could save work time."[71]

One example of these advances is the European fishing industry. Before the Black Death, fishermen routinely came ashore to salt the fish they had recently caught, which would preserve them for a long time. Then, they sailed back out and caught more fish. Just like in the rest of the economy, this process no longer had enough people to keep it up, so the number of fish that could be caught and preserved was too small to sustain people's needs. Trying to find solutions to this problem, "in 1380, Dutch fishermen perfected a method of salting, drying, and storing their catch aboard [their] ship," Gottfried wrote. "This allowed them to stay at sea longer, sail farther from shore, and bring home more fish."[72]

One of the most important and influential technological advances of all time also occurred during this pots-plague period: the invention of the printing press. Commonly referred to as printing with movable type, the press immediately revolutionized the production, distribution, and consumption of literature and other written materials. Indeed, few inventions in history have transformed the world as much as the press. Before movable type, the only way to produce a book was to write it by hand; these kinds of books are known as manuscripts. The manuscript then had to be very carefully copied by hand over and over again. Before the plague, this job was done by thousands of highly trained individuals called copyists. Bookmakers in Europe were also left without a strong workforce after the plague, but the demand for books was higher than ever. Historian David Herlihy explained,

The growth of universities in the twelfth and thirteenth centuries and the expanding numbers of literate laymen [average people] generated a strong demand for books. Numerous scribes were employed to copy manuscripts. At Paris, for example, in the [1200s], manuscripts were divided into [sections] and given to separate scribes, who assiduously [carefully] reproduced them. The parts were then combined into the finished book. As long as wages were low, this method of reproduction based on intensive human labor was satisfactory enough. But the late medieval population plunge raised labor costs and also raised the premium to be claimed by the one who could devise a cheaper way of reproducing books. Johann Gutenberg's invention of printing on the basis of movable metal type in 1453 was only the culmination [result] of many experiments carried on across the previous century. His genius was in finding a way to combine several technologies into the new art.[73]

The Black Death also improved medical knowledge and techniques during the late 14th century. People were painfully aware that their doctors had not had the knowledge or ability to stop the plague. Later outbreaks of the disease in the 1390s and early 1400s only reinforced the need for advances in medical science.

Many European doctors took their failures seriously and admitted they did not know enough about the human body. To fix this shortcoming, Pope Clement VI reversed the Church's law regarding the dissection of dead humans. Called cadavers, dead human bodies had been off-limits for educational purposes for a long time. Studying cadavers brought about major new advances in the emerging science of anatomy, which is the study of the human body. There was also a new interest and confidence in direct surgical methods. European universities rarely taught surgery in the pre-plague years, but some began adding surgical instruction in the century following the plague.

The invention of the printing press was one positive outcome of the plague in Europe.

ART INSPIRED BY DEATH

One of the most famous and stunning European pieces of artwork inspired by the Black Death is a fresco (painting done on wet plaster) by the Italian master Francesco Traini in 1350. It is appropriately titled *The Triumph of Death*. Noted scholar Barbara W. Tuchman provided this vivid description of the work:

> In Traini's fresco, Death swoops through the air toward a group of carefree, young, and beautiful noblemen and ladies who … converse and flirt and entertain each other with books and music in a fragrant grove of orange trees. A scroll warns that "no shield of wisdom or riches, nobility or prowess" can protect them from the blows of the Approaching One [death] … In a heap of corpses nearby lie crowned rulers, a Pope in a tiara, [and] a knight, tumbled together with the bodies of the poor, while angels and devils in the sky contend for [fight over] the miniature naked figures that represent their souls. A wretched group of lepers, cripples, and beggars … implore [beg] Death for deliverance.[1]

1. Barbara W. Tuchman, *A Distant Mirror: The Calamitous 14th Century*. New York, NY: Ballantine, 1996, p. 130.

Traini portrayed death approaching everyone, regardless of their wealth or social status, in his 1350 fresco.

Education and Learning

European higher education changed following the Black Death in more ways than just the inclusion of teaching surgical methods. One immediately noticeable difference was a sudden decrease in the number of qualified instructors of any subject. Another was a significant drop-off in student attendance at most universities. This is not surprising; the plague killed people from every level of society. Even after the spread of death, people often had more important things on their minds than continuing their education.

The literate and highly educated members of society, who made up only a small percentage of the population, were very concerned by these trends. Charles IV, ruler of the central European nation known as the Holy Roman Empire, wanted to save "precious knowledge which the mad rage of pestilential death has stifled throughout the wide realms of the world."[74] He and other leading figures were worried that universities, and maybe even learning itself, might not survive the devastation left by the plague. This motivated them to look for qualified replacements for the lost teachers wherever possible.

Additionally, several new universities were established in the era around the Black Death. Among the more famous and long-lasting were Trinity College in Cambridge, England, and Charles IV's personal project, the University of Prague in the modern-day Czech Republic.

The great plague also indirectly affected learning by making literature easier to read and more available to the people. Some modern scholars point out that before the Black Death, teachers and priests (who copied and preserved many writings) used Latin for most documents. In the era after the plague, there was a switch to writing in languages used by more Europeans, such as Italian, French, German, and English. Explaining this theory, historian William H. McNeill wrote that "the decay of Latin as a *lingua franca* [shared language] among the educated men of western Europe was hastened [sped up] by the die-off of clerics and teachers who knew enough Latin to keep that ancient tongue alive."[75]

This theory is one more way that European languages, culture, ideas, and values, which later spread across the globe, were shaped by the Black Death.

THE PAST AND PRESENT OF THE PLAGUE

By 1351, the Black Death had largely ended, but the destruction it left behind was astounding. At least one-third, and maybe even more, of Europe's human population died from the disease, and many aspects of life for those remaining were changed forever. However, Europe had not seen the last of this terrible disease. It returned numerous times, and although each return was smaller than the initial outbreak, the plague always took awful tolls. It killed thousands, spread fear, and devastated local economies.

Despite some advances in medicine and science, the plague kept coming back because doctors and other authorities still did not know what caused the disease or how it spread. They simply could not figure out why it kept returning. At the time, the only thing they could do was hope the plague stayed away and try their best to stay alive if it did strike.

Today, very few people have to worry about the plague. Fortunately, medical science made huge advances in the early modern era that provided a basic understanding that most diseases are caused by germs, including the germ called *Yersinia pestis* that was responsible for causing the Black Death. Although this germ still exists, it no longer poses the terrible threat to individuals and society that it once did. This does not mean that it has been forgotten, however. The Black Death remains a dark reminder of the potential horrors of widespread epidemics.

A Cycle of Horror

Though more recent disease outbreaks have created even more massive death tolls, the true devastation of the Black Death is that it killed more than

35 percent of Europe's total population. By comparison, the influenza outbreak of 1918 to 1919 killed 20 to 40 million people, roughly 3 percent of the world's population. For a society with almost none of the medical knowledge of the 20th century, the bubonic plague outbreaks that struck Europe in the centuries immediately following the Black Death were still incredibly frightening and destructive.

The first major reappearance of the disease after 1351 was a decade later. In 1361, the *pestis secunda* (second plague), arrived in Europe. "The return of plague was a nightmare reborn," historian Robert Gottfried wrote.

While primarily an attack of bubonic plague, and not as severe as the Black Death, the pestis secunda was still one of the most lethal epidemics in history. Many observers ... believed it was especially deadly for select groups, including the young—those born after the Black Death [who had no immunity]—and the landed upper classes.[76]

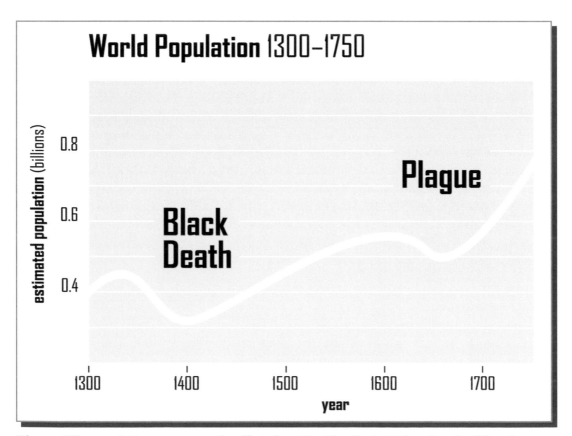

The world's population was severely affected not just by the initial outbreak of the plague, but also by the smaller outbreaks that followed.

Eyewitnesses to the disaster claim that thousands of nobles, bishops, and children were killed by the plague in 1361. Based on contemporary documents and historical research, it is estimated that 10 to 20 percent of Europe's population was killed in the second plague.

After that, the plague seemed to just keep returning. Every few years, it reappeared, sometimes in one country, other times in several, forming a kind of plague cycle. England, for instance, had significant outbreaks in 1369, 1379 to 1383, 1390 to 1391, 1405 to 1406, 1411 to 1412, 1426 to 1429, and several other times in the three centuries that followed.

Although none of these outbreaks reproduced the gigantic death toll of the Black Death, the despair and suffering of families and victims were no less intense. During a 1471 outbreak in England, a man visiting London sent a letter to his relatives in Norfolk. He wrote, "I pray you send me word if any of our friends or well-willers be dead, for I fear that there is great death … [in] Norfolk; for I ensure you, it is the most universal death that ever I [witnessed] in England."[77]

The horror of this seemingly endless cycle of plague and death in Europe can be seen in various surviving statistics. As just one example, Northern Germany had 179 local villages in 1300, before the first onset of plague. In 1500, after numerous outbreaks of the disease in the region, only 33 of those villages still existed. The rest had been totally wiped out by the disease and abandoned.

EARTHQUAKE THEORY

Well after the terrible Black Death of the 1300s, smaller epidemics of the disease struck Europe. Most people continued to accept nonsensical theories about the causes of these diseases. One of the most common theories was that earthquakes and diseases had the same cause. Although this seems silly today, people at the time were just as ignorant about the causes of earthquakes as they were about the causes of epidemics. One common explanation for earthquakes was that they happened when dangerous fumes trapped beneath the earth suddenly exploded onto the surface. These same fumes, which were considered impure, were then released into the atmosphere, where they caused diseases, including the bubonic plague.

How Did the Plague Stop?

Major outbreaks of bubonic plague eventually slowed, and the disease became considerably less lethal. Over time, people did develop some precautions against it. In the early 1700s in what is now Hungary, for example, hundreds of checkpoints were set up and manned by thousands of guards.

These acted as quarantines by limiting traders and other human traffic moving into Europe from the East. Another theory for the reduction of plague in Europe is that the original bacteria that caused the disease evolved into a less deadly form.

The most important factor in humanity's victory over plague is the 19th-century discovery that germs cause disease and the later identification of the specific microbe that causes plague. When combined with better health practices in much of Europe in the 19th century, scientific knowledge definitively helped minimize the death toll from many harmful diseases, including plague.

The key period during which many of these breakthroughs were made began in 1854. That year, French scientist Louis Pasteur successfully demonstrated that germs cause certain foods to change their chemical composition. Scientists were aware of the existence of germs before that, but they had assumed that these tiny organisms played no major role in nature. In his experiments, Pasteur showed that they had been invisible but active throughout history. Next, Pasteur and some other scientists set out to confirm something they already suspected—that germs not only cause disease, but can protect against it as well.

Pasteur found his proof by chance. He was studying cholera, a deadly disease common in chickens and other birds, and he had to obtain some samples of the germs and use them for experiments. Every two weeks, he would inject the bacteria into his laboratory animals, allow them to get sick, and then extract the disease again. This ensured that his supply of germs was always fresh and strong. After he went on vacation and let one batch of germs sit for more than a month, he tried to circulate it and get some new samples. However, because sitting on a lab table for so long had weakened the cholera germs, they did not cause an infection. Confused, Pasteur continued investigating why this occurred. Eventually, he found that if a very weak group of bacteria is introduced to an animal, it will no longer be affected by a full-strength attack by that same disease.

This was a major breakthrough for medical science. Not only was the germ theory of disease proven by these experiments, but Pasteur was also bringing humanity closer to the ability to effectively fight deadly sicknesses. His work was remarkable because he also found a way to consistently weaken the groups of lethal bacteria by exposing them to extreme heat.

He used the techniques he learned from cholera to develop a vaccine for another common disease: anthrax. Other scientists pushed Pasteur to do a large demonstration to publicly prove his theory. On May 5, 1881, with both scientists and newspaper reporters watching, Pasteur and his assistants injected 25 sheep with their anthrax vaccine while 25 other sheep received

French scientist Louis Pasteur's discoveries about germs and disease helped stop the spread of bubonic plague and other deadly diseases.

no vaccine. The next step was to give the vaccinated sheep a few weeks to build up immunity. Then, on May 31, Pasteur injected all 50 sheep with full-strength anthrax germs.

Many people, including Pasteur's critics, were unsure of what to expect from this new science. However, on June 2, nearly all of the unvaccinated sheep died of anthrax, while all of the vaccinated ones remained healthy. Pasteur had shown clearly that anthrax bacteria caused the disease and further, that a vaccine made from the same bacteria could make an animal immune from anthrax.

Scientists all across the world were inspired by Pasteur's revolutionary experiment, and they began isolating and studying the germs that cause a number of harmful diseases. It was one of Pasteur's associates, Alexandre Yersin, who isolated the bubonic plague bacterium in 1894, which is why it is named in his honor. Yersin also tried to discover the ways that the disease was transferred to humans but was unable to confirm any. Not long afterward, French scientist Paul-Louis Simond, who worked at the Pasteur

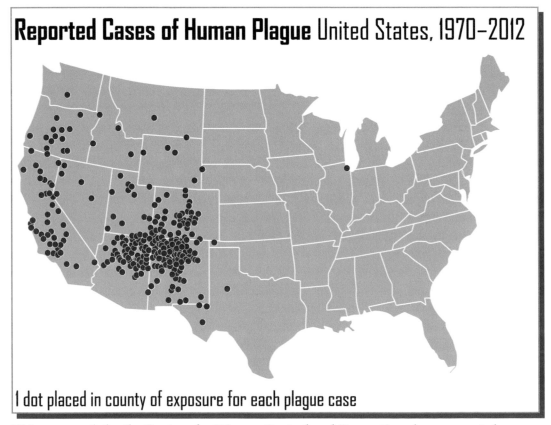

Reported Cases of Human Plague United States, 1970–2012

1 dot placed in county of exposure for each plague case

This map made by the Centers for Disease Control and Prevention shows reported cases of plague in the United States over a period of 42 years.

Institute in Paris, found that the main carrier of the deadly plague was the rat flea.

Thanks in large part to Pasteur, Yersin, Simond, and other modern medical researchers, the plague no longer delivers as much misery and death as it did in past ages. However, it is important to point out that the disease still exists. Incidents of the plague, though rare, still pop up from time to time.

In 2002, for example, a couple from Santa Fe, New Mexico, decided to spend a few days in New York City. They did not know that they been bitten by plague-carrying fleas in their own backyard. After coming down with some initial symptoms, including fever and tiredness, they checked into a hospital in New York. Though the wife recovered quickly, her husband had developed septicemic plague—the most lethal form of the disease. However, because of the amazing advances to modern medicine since the time of the Black Death, they both survived.

A Haunting Memory

The effects of the Black Death are still present in our society today. The memory haunts popular culture and is often used to represent God's wrath

AN IMPORTANT DISCOVERY

French scientist Paul-Louis Simond, who established that the rat flea was the main carrier of bubonic plague, later recalled his excitement when his experiment was successful in confirming his suspicions:

Without delay I proceeded to the experiment I had in mind since the time ... I had discovered Yersin's bacillus in the digestive tract of fleas taken from plague-ridden rats. I prepared [for the experiment] ... I was fortunate enough to catch a plague infected rat in the home of a plague victim. In the rat's fur there were several fleas running around ...

That day, 2 June 1898, I felt an emotion [of excitement that is hard to express] in the face of the thought that I had uncovered a secret that had tortured man since the appearance of plague in the world. The mechanism of the propagation [spread] of plague includes the transporting of the microbe by rat and man, its transmission from rat to rat, from human to human, from rat to human and from human to rat by parasites [fleas].[1]

1. Quoted in Marc Simond et al., "Paul-Louis Simond and His Discovery of Plague Transmission by Rat Fleas: A Centenary," *Journal of the Royal Society of Medicine*, February 1998, p. 102.

and widespread death. In many works of art, such as novels, plays, poems, paintings, and movies, the Black Death seems to take on supernatural qualities. "As the actual plague recedes into history," one modern researcher observed, "the memory of it becomes increasingly symbolic, like something from a dream, a subject for mythological interpretations."[78]

Although we view our modern-day society as advanced and immune to such tragedies, experts warn that we should realize that our society, too, has limitations. Disease and the natural world are always advancing, just as our society advances, and the next wave of frightening disease could come from anywhere. Continuing to research and explore things as new discoveries are made is important to the survival of the human race as a whole. In the words of the American historian William H. McNeill:

> Everyone can surely agree that a fuller comprehension of humanity's ever-changing place in the balance of nature ought to be part of our understanding of history, and no one can doubt that the role of infectious diseases in the natural balance has been and remains of key importance.[79]

Notes

Introduction:
A Terrible Event in History

1. Giovanni Boccaccio, *Decameron*, trans. J.G. Nichols. New York, NY: Knopf, 2009, p. 8.
2. Boccaccio, *Decameron*, p. 10.
3. Robert S. Gottfried, *The Black Death: Natural and Human Disaster in Medieval Europe*. New York, NY: Macmillan, 1985, pp. 134–135.
4. Isaiah 37:33–36 (New King James Version).
5. William H. McNeill, "Infectious Alternatives: The Plague that Saved Jerusalem," in Robert Cowley, ed., *What If: The World's Foremost Military Historians Imagine What Might Have Been*. New York, NY: Berkley, 1999, p. 9.
6. Cowley, *What If*, p. 2.
7. Thucydides, *History of the Peloponnesian War*, trans. Rex Warner. New York, NY: Penguin, 1972, pp. 152–153.
8. Procopius, *History of the Wars*, trans. H.B. Dewing. Cambridge, MA: Harvard University Press, 1935, pp. 451–452

Chapter One:
Black Death Beginnings

9. Alfred J. Bollet, *Plagues and Poxes: The Impact of Human History on Epidemic Disease*. New York, NY: Demos, 2004, p. 20.
10. Quoted in Rosemary Horrox, *The Black Death*. Manchester, UK: Manchester University Press, 1994, p. 17.
11. Philip Ziegler, *The Black Death*. New York, NY: Harper Perennial, 2009, p. 5.
12. Quoted in David Herlihy, *The Black Death and the Transformation of the West*, ed. Samuel K. Cohn Jr. Cambridge, MA: Harvard University Press, 1997, p. 24.
13. Quoted in Johannes Nohl, *The Black Death: A Chronicle of the Plague*, trans. C.H. Clarke. Yardly, PA: Westholme, 2006, pp. 18–19.
14. Quoted in Nohl, *The Black Death*, p. 18.
15. Boccaccio, *Decameron*, p. 12.
16. Boccaccio, *Decameron*, pp. 11–12.
17. Boccaccio, *Decameron*, pp. 12–13.
18. Boccaccio, *Decameron*, pp. 15–16.
19. Jean de Venette, *The Chronicle of Jean de Venette*, trans. Jean Birdsall. New York, NY: Columbia University Press, 1953, pp. 48–49.

20. Quoted in Otto Friedrich, *The End of the World: A History.* New York, NY: Fromm International, 1994, p. 121.
21. Joseph P. Byrne, *Encyclopedia of the Black Death.* Santa Barbara, CA: ABC-CLIO 2012, p. 245.
22. Quoted in Toni Mount, *A Year in the Life of Medieval England.* Gloucestershire, UK: Amberley Publishing, 2016.
23. Quoted in Friedrich, *The End of the World*, p. 125.
24. Quoted in Barbara W. Tuchman, *A Distant Mirror: The Calamitous 14th Century.* New York, NY: Ballantine, 1996, p. 99.

Chapter Two:
A Plague of Terror and Panic

25. De Venette, *The Chronicle of Jean de Venette*, p. 48.
26. Quoted in Horrox, *The Black Death*, pp. 160–161.
27. Quoted in Horrox, *The Black Death*, pp. 113–114.
28. Tuchman, *A Distant Mirror*, p. 109.
29. "Town of Pistoia: Ordinances for Sanitation in a Time of Mortality," Institute for Advanced Technology in the Humanities. www2.iath.virginia.edu/osheim/pistoia.html.
30. Quoted in Ziegler, *The Black Death*, p. 38.
31. Quoted in Sylvia Lettice Thrupp, *Change in Medieval Society: Europe North of the Alps, 1050–1500.* Toronto, ON, Canada: University of Toronto Press, 1988, p. 214.
32. James C. Giblin, *When Plague Strikes: The Black Death, Smallpox, AIDS.* New York, NY: HarperCollins, 1997, pp. 32–33.
33. Quoted in Horrox, *The Black Death*, p. 45.
34. Tuchman, *A Distant Mirror*, p. 116.
35. Quoted in Horrox, *The Black Death*, p. 222.
36. Quoted in Horrox, *The Black Death*, p. 208.
37. Quoted in Paul Halsall, ed.,"Jewish History Sourcebook: The Black Death and the Jews 1348–1349 CE," Internet History Sourcebooks Project. www.fordham.edu/halsall/jewish/1348-jewsblackdeath.html.
38. Quoted in Halsall, "Jewish History Sourcebook."
39. Quoted in Ziegler, *The Black Death*, p. 67.
40. Quoted in Friedrich, *The End of the World*, p. 126.
41. Quoted in Friedrich, *The End of the World*, p. 126.
42. Quoted in Friedrich, *The End of the World*, p. 129.
43. Friedrich, *The End of the World*, p. 134.

Chapter Three:
Black Death Facts

44. Herlihy, *The Black Death and the Transformation of the West*, pp. 20–21.
45. Giblin, *When Plague Strikes*, p. 14.
46. Giblin, *When Plague Strikes*, pp. 11–12.

47. Quoted in Nohl, *The Black Death*, p. 20.
48. Bollet, *Plagues and Poxes*, p. 21.
49. Giblin, *When Plague Strikes*, p. 13.
50. Ziegler, *The Black Death*, p. 18.
51. Gottfried, *The Black Death*, p. 4.

Chapter Four:
Economic Effects of the Plague

52. Quoted in Herlihy, *The Black Death and the Transformation of the West*, p. 41.
53. Gottfried, *The Black Death*, p. 94.
54. Matteo Villani, *Universal Chronicle*, excerpted in Perry M. Rogers, *Aspects of Western Civilization*. Upper Saddler River, NJ: Prentice Hall, 2000, pp. 353–365.
55. Quoted in Herlihy, *The Black Death and the Transformation of the West*, pp. 48–49.
56. Quoted in Rogers, *Aspects of Western Civilization*, p. 365.
57. Herlihy, *The Black Death and the Transformation of the West*, p. 47.
58. Herlihy, *The Black Death and the Transformation of the West*, p. 48.
59. Ziegler, *The Black Death*, p. 199.
60. Quoted in Knighton, *The Chronicle of Henry Knighton*.
61. Quoted in Paul Halsall, ed., "Medieval Source Book: Jean Froissart on the Jacquerie, 1358," Internet History Sourcebooks Project. sourcebooks.fordham.edu/halsall/source/froissart2.asp.
62. Friedrich Lutge, "Germany: The Black Death and a Structural Revolution in Socioeconomic History," in *The Black Death: A Turning Point in History?* ed. William M. Bowsky. New York, NY: Holt, Rinehart and Winston, 1978, p. 84.

Chapter Five:
Impacts on Culture

63. Friedrich, *The End of the World*, pp. 136–137.
64. De Venette, *The Chronicle of Jean de Venette*, p. 51.
65. Gottfried, *The Black Death*, p. 89.
66. Johan Huizinga, *The Waning of the Middle Ages*. Mineola, NY: Dover, 1998, p. 134.
67. Tuchman, *A Distant Mirror*, p. 129.
68. Ziegler, *The Black Death*, p. 279.
69. Giblin, *When Plague Strikes*, p. 43.
70. Gottfried, *The Black Death*, p. 142.
71. Gottfried, *The Black Death*, p. 142.
72. Gottfried, *The Black Death*, p. 142.
73. Herlihy, *The Black Death and the Transformation of the West*, pp. 49–50.
74. Quoted in Tuchman, *A Distant Mirror*, p. 124.
75. William H. McNeill, *Plagues and Peoples*. New York, NY: Anchor, 1998, p. 193.

Epilogue:
The Past and Present of the Plague

76. Gottfried, *The Black Death*, p. 130.
77. Quoted in John Fenn, *Paston Letters: Original Letters Written During the Reigns of Henry VI, Edward the IV, and Richard III*, vol. 1. London, UK: Charles Knight, 1840, p. 63.
78. Friedrich, *The End of the World*, pp. 137–138.
79. McNeill, *Plagues and Peoples*, p. 23.

For More Information

Books

Boccaccio, Giovanni. *Decameron*. Translated by J.G. Nichols. New York, NY: Knopf, 2009.

> Boccaccio's work is the best-known primary source documenting the horrors of the Black Death as seen by an eyewitness.

Byrne, Joseph Patrick. *Encyclopedia of the Black Death*. Santa Barbara, CA: ABC-CLIO, 2012.

> This new encyclopedia allows readers of any experience level to find out more about the many aspects of the Black Death.

Currie, Stephen. *The Black Death*. San Diego, CA: ReferencePoint Press, 2013.

> From the causes of the plague to story of its progression through Europe, this book covers the interesting timeline of the Black Death.

Kelly, John. *The Great Mortality: An Intimate History of the Black Death*. New York, NY: Harper Perennial, 2006.

> This is an excellent overview of the onset, devastation, and effects of the Black Death.

Martin, Sean. *The Black Death*. Secaucus, NJ: Chartwell, 2009.

> This book provides a short but fact-filled presentation of the basic facts about the Black Death and is perfect for beginners to the study of this subject.

Scott, Susan, and Christopher Duncan. *Return to the Black Death: The World's Greatest Serial Killer*. New York, NY: Wiley, 2005.

> This book discusses the 1300s version of the plague and considers the possibility that it might return in the near future.

Ziegler, Philip. *The Black Death*. New York, NY: Harper Perennial, 2009.

> This book offers a comprehensive and thoughtful study by one of the world's leading experts on the subject.

Websites

Black Death
www.britannica.com/event/Black-Death
> This encyclopedia entry not only has a brief overview of the various aspects of the Black Death, it also includes relevant pictures and links to other related entries.

Black Death: Facts and Summary
www.history.com/topics/black-death
> This site has information and interactive media that help users learn about the Black Death in an easy-to-understand format.

Insecta Inspecta: The Black Death
www.insecta-inspecta.com/fleas/bdeath/Black.html
> This website offers information about the fleas responsible for the spread of plague, including pictures of people affected by the disease.

Plague Homepage
www.cdc.gov/plague/
> Produced by the U.S. government, this website has detailed information on the plague and its history worldwide.

Your 60-Second Guide to the Black Death
www.historyextra.com/feature/your-60-second-guide-facts-black-death-how-when-why
> Brief but informative, this fun website has a convenient question-answer format that makes understanding all of its information easy.

Index

population
    pre-plague increase, 15
    return to pre-plague levels, 9, 43
prayer as treatment, 39, 57–58
prevention
    personal immunity, 54
    sanitation, 39, 54
printing press, 80–81
Procopius, 9, 12
Pulex irritans, 53

Q
quarantine measures, 32–33, 87–88

R
rat fleas, 47, 50, 91
rats, 47–48, 53, 91
rebellions
    in England, 68
    in France, 66–68
religious effects
    crisis of faith, 75, 77
    increase in fees, 63–64
Richard II (king of England), 68–69
Roman Empire, 12, 56
route of plague, 16–19
Russia, 26–27

S
Saint Anthony's fire, 15
sanitation, 39, 54
scapegoats, 33, 39
septicemic plague, 53, 91
serfs, 60, 62
Siena, Italy, 28
Simond, Paul-Louis, 90–91

smallpox, 12
social effects, 71–73
Sparta, 11
symptoms
    classic, 48–49
    described by eyewitnesses, 9, 12,
      19, 49, 87

T
Tartars, 17
technological effects, 78–80
Thucydides, 11–12
trade, 16–18, 63
Traini, Francesco, 82–83
treatment, 32, 45–46, 55, 57–58
Trinity College, 84
Triumph of Death (Traini), 82–83
Tuchman, Barbara W., 31, 37, 74, 82

U
universities, 77, 80–81, 84
University of Prague, 84

V
vaccines, 88, 90
de Venette, Jean, 24, 29–30, 72–73
Venice, Italy, 32–33, 37
Villani, Matteo, 63–64

W
Wat Tyler's Rebellion, 68–69

X
Xenopsylla cheopis, 47

Y

Z

Picture Credits

About the Author

Emily Mahoney is the author of more than a dozen nonfiction books for young readers on various topics. She has a master's degree in literacy from the University at Buffalo and a bachelor's degree from Canisius College in adolescent education and English. She currently teaches reading to middle school students and loves watching her students learn how to become better readers and writers. She enjoys reading, Pilates, yoga, and spending time with family and friends. She lives with her husband in Buffalo, New York, where she was born and raised.